UFO:

END-TIME

DELUSION

UFO:
END-TIME
DELUSION

by
David Allen Lewis
and Robert Shreckhise

NewLeaf
Press

SECOND EDITION
1992

ISBN: 0-89221-213-6
Library of Congress Catalog Number: 91-61713
All Scripture quotations are from the King James Version unless otherwise noted.

Contents

INTRODUCTION

This treatise has been a long time in coming. It is time for it now. After readers consider this book, it will be debated whether UFOs are real or not. We believe they are real. But what is reality? Is it only that which our five senses perceive?

Even if you think that UFOs are a result of hysteria, or that they are hoaxes, still this book will help you understand one of the most amazing phenomena of all time. One could say that debating whether they are real or not misses the point.

Whether UFOs are real or not, the idea is real. It lives in people's minds. It is a part of both secular humanity's and the New Age movement's belief structure. People believe in UFOs. Over twenty million Americans have reported seeing UFOs. It is estimated that twice that number have not reported sightings because they fear ridicule. That people believe in UFOs is important, for people's beliefs dictate the way they conduct themselves. Belief forms the basis of one's outlook on life. It provides a model by which one views and interprets reality. If the alleged messages that contactees are receiving are true, then the Bible is not true. God is not what or who we think He is. Christianity must be radically altered to fit the new paradigm (model, pattern by which we perceive reality). Mention UFOs in some circles and you will be greeted with polite chuckles and comments about "little green men from Mars." But bright people in government, the scientific community, the military, and even religious circles are taking the subject seriously. Firmly implanted in people's mind is the belief in UFOs and the idea that they may soon be revealing themselves to humanity — whether for good or for hostility.

There is no longer any reasonable doubt in our minds

that modern UFO manifestations are supernatural in origin and activity. This statement is the result of almost forty years of research. This explanation will not only suit people who already have confidence in the Bible, but also will have strong appeal for any honest inquirer. It will lead many people to a new respect for the Holy Scriptures. We are ready to document and demonstrate that our position is accurate.

Since 1952, we have researched by reading, interviewing people claiming personal sightings, and communicating with some who claim "close encounter of the third kind (CE-3)."

HOW THIS BOOK WAS WRITTEN

I was impressed with Robert L. Shreckhise's suggestion that his topic for the Annual Springfield Fall Prophecy Conference might be the subject of UFOs. In further conversation I suggested that he write a lengthy paper which we could have printed in booklet form for the conference.

I noted that I had researched UFO phenomena since 1952 and would be glad to lend him materials for his study. Then an inspiration came to me, *Why just a booklet — why not a full-sized book?*

Pastor Shreckhise agreed to write a first draft manuscript of the book, except for the chapter based on my interview of those involved in the Arkansas incident. I sent Bob my extensive library — boxes of books, files, lecture notes, lecture tapes, and interview tapes — for his use in preparing the first draft.

This work would not be finished at this time without his help. I requested that he base the book on my lecture outlines, and that my basic eight-point position statement form the framework of the manuscript. Robert was to be free to bring all his expertise and knowledge to the work; this he admirably did. The publisher was amazed that he got the manuscript ready in such a short time.

Bob sent me a 3.5 inch computer disk containing the

entire book. This allowed me to go into each chapter file and edit easily. I wish to personally thank Robert Shreckhise for assisting me in this work. It is as much a product of his work as of my own. It has truly been a joint effort.

David Allen Lewis
Springfield, Missouri

CHAPTER ONE

CLOSE ENCOUNTERS

AUTHOR DAVID LEWIS BEARS WITNESS

A REMARKABLE PREDICTION

In 1952 I became interested in the subject of UFOs. While attending college in Missouri, I became aware of reported sightings in the area. I wondered what they were. This was the beginning of almost forty years of research: reading hundreds of books, conducting interviews, corresponding, watching videos, and examining photographs. In 1952 I had already formulated a biblical and scientific theory on the nature of UFOs. In 1955 I shared it from the pulpit of a church where Rev. Harley Hansel was the minister. After the meeting he and I discussed UFOs for hours at his home. I quoted from M. K. Jessup's book on UFOs and in the following days we read the book and talked about how close some of his ideas were to mine.

Thus, in St. Ignace, Michigan, I first publicly predicted that a new theory—one with a cloak of scientific credibility — would delude mankind about the nature of God. I predicted it would have the same impact as Darwin's "evolution": to confuse the world about the origin of human life and the nature of man. I predicted that as people would ponder ancient wonders like the pyramids, someone would propose that early man was too primitive to do these things unaided. It would be suggested that aliens visited Earth and superimposed their technology on Earthling efforts. Thus the wonders of the ancient world came to be. Further, I predicted that someone would come along and suggest that there is no God in the biblical sense, but that early man's inability to comprehend life on other planets, interstellar space vehicles, and alien beings led them to invent mythical and legendary explanations for these phenomena. This is how "myths" about gods, devils, angels, and demons came to be.

Just suppose, however, that the Bible is historically accurate. Most people who deny that it is have never read the Bible through or looked at the body of scientific evidence testifying to its accuracy. If the Bible were true, there would be an entirely different approach to interpreting alleged alien visits, both ancient and modern. We think that we deserve a day in court. We urge a thoughtful examination of the critically important ideas presented here. The destiny of our world and the lives of millions of people are at stake.

Last week Rev. Harley Hansel was in my home. I asked him if he remembered our discussion, so many years ago, in St. Ignace. He said, "David, how could I forget it? Don't you remember? We stayed up all night talking about it!" Al Jukeri will remember that I presented my case to his group in Charlevoux, Michigan later. Herbert David Kolenda and Dan Kolenda will also recall my early lectures on the subject. After that initial series of talks, I only occasionally could be prevailed upon to present the message. It was not yet the time for a general exposure of my ideas. Now the time has come when it must be made available to everyone.

Years ago, I was invited to give a lecture series on world affairs and the Bible at a church located in Twenty-Nine Palms, California. Rev. C. C. Krake was the minister. Since the church was near a Marine base, many service people attended the meetings. An officer invited me to a breakfast at the base with the commanding general and officers of the base. At the breakfast I was asked if I would like to witness a fire power demonstration of weaponry far out in the desert. At the demonstration I was seated with some officers, including the general. The weapons exhibited in operation were truly awesome. Laser-guided missiles, shoulder-held rocket launchers, the latest tanks, and diverse ordnance were put through their paces.

Most amazing of all was the Harrier aircraft. At that time there was no public awareness that the "jump jet" was in existence. I was even allowed to photograph it both in the air and on the ground. Without any announcement it came roaring from out of the desert behind us, and then it seemed to slam on its brakes in mid-air! This non-propeller, pure jet craft literally hovered above and in front of us. It could rotate, back up, creep forward, rise straight up, and lower itself — straight down. The officer I was seated by turned to me and said, "You know, I bet it is experimental craft like this that are responsible for these UFO sightings." He did not know of my interest; it was just a casual remark. I replied, "Yes, I believe that accounts for some, and maybe a good share of them."

I knew from my research that some reported UFOs turn out to be IFOs (identifiable flying objects), such as weather balloons, mirages, hallucinations, LSD trips, and hoaxes (fake pictures). But there are many sightings that cannot be identified. Further, the characteristics of true UFOs, as investigated by credible scientists like the late J. Allen Hynek, manifest properties that cannot be credited to anything known to man. It is the latter in which we are interested.

I believe that UFOs are real (provided you allow my definition of reality). I believe they are from an occult or paranormal source. Hynek believed this. Vallee also believes this. My research has led me to a further conclusion, and that is that they are evil. Humanity must be warned of the malevolent intentions of the "aliens." That is the purpose of this book. While some contacts have been friendly and some hostile, they are all from the same source and they mean to destroy all human life on this planet.

We are not defenseless, but ignorance and misconception are powerful weapons against us. Deception is currently the "alien's" most effective tool. We intend to unmask the delusion. We will furnish you the means to combat it. Humanity needs a rescue program right now. *UFO — End -Time Delusion* provides a basis for that action program.

SIGNS OF THE TIMES

Maybe you will disagree with us. Possibly you will not believe that UFOs are real, and you may think we have missed the boat. You may find it hard to believe that they are paranormal or psychic in nature and origin. Despite that, this book still makes a valid contribution to the understanding of this transitional era in which we live. Everyone senses that we are living in a time of monumental change. The New Age movement looks to a paradigm shift around the year 2000. Some Christians believe that Christ will come back then. The year 2000 is being used as a symbol or physical logo by politicians, corporations, environmental agencies, and New Agers. There is a soap named Lever 2000. The airport in my home town has a big sign with the 2000 logo. I have a picture of President Bush standing in front of a huge 2000 logo. I see it everywhere. (See Chapter 1 of *Prophecy 2000,* New Leaf Press.)

These things are important. Symbolism and perceptions powerfully affect the actions of mankind. The fact that millions of people believe in UFOs, aliens, and possible contact makes the subject important. Clever, designing politicians will manage to use this perception for manipulative purposes. If we turn out to be right, and we firmly believe that we are, the consequences are so far-reaching that it will affect the life of every man, woman, and child on planet Earth.

Dr. J. Allen Hynek was undoubtedly the foremost researcher of the UFO phenomena from a scientific standpoint. Frequently he was consulted by the government and the military for analysis of UFO data and sightings and was a major contributor to the Air Force Project Blue Book (UFO research). It was he who developed the "close encounters" terminology.

A "close encounter of the first kind (CE-1)" describes the experience of anyone who has seen an unidentified flying object, usually from a distance.

A "close encounter of the second kind (CE-2)" describes the experience of a person who has seen physical evidence left behind or caused by a UFO occurrence. It also fits the experience of one who has had physical evidence inflicted upon him (sunburned appearance, radiation, and so on).

A "close encounter of the third kind (CE-3)" involves actual contact and/or communication with an alleged alien or extraterrestrial being(s). An amazing number of people make such claims. Some have written books and articles about their experiences. Many have been interviewed by NASA, the U.S. Air Force, or MUFON (Mutual UFO Network). Many people in our government, the military, and in the space agency take this UFO business very seriously!

PARANORMAL CONNECTION

Without exception, every person claiming a CE-3 contact that I have researched, corresponded with, or met had one thing in common. Each had a prior connection to metaphysical activity or cults. Some had been in devil worship, witchcraft, psychic phenomena, New Age, channeling, and so on. (We will mention the Andreasson case as a possible exception.) Those involved in direct contact with UFO aliens already had a connection to the dark side of the supernatural world.

There are many born-again Christians of our acquaintance who have had CE-1 experiences — a mere sighting of a UFO. Some Christians have had a CE-2 — where some physical evidence or change is left behind, indicating that the sighting was real.

We recently interviewed two Christians in Arkansas for about six hours altogether. Their experience would fall in the CE-2 category. It is significant, I believe, that no Christian of our acquaintance has had a CE-3 (direct encounter with alleged E.T.). Now, what do you make of that?

For the plan of the deceivers to succeed, it seems likely that they will try to change this situation. It is not tolerable to them that a significant body of people is resistant to the new paradigm the UFOs present. Somehow it must be made to appear that born-again Christians also have direct contact, whether it is friendly or hostile in nature. They, too, must testify to having been taken on board a spacecraft, physically examined, assaulted sexually, or perhaps given a "trip" out into space to see the solar system. Be aware of this factor and you will be armed against the deception and the deceivers themselves. Was this the level of deception attempted in the case of the two women in Arkansas? As you read the interview with Joanne Wilson in this book, you will be able to draw your own conclusions.

OUTER SPACE DECEPTION WILL BE EXPOSED

Many in the New Age movement believe that planet Earth is a living being, a goddess named Gaia. They believe that Gaia (Earth) is communicating with "Ascended Masters of the Hierarchy of the universe." They believe that soon our "space brothers" will raise a human leader from our midst whom they will endow with supernormal powers and wisdom. This man will lead the world to global government and world peace. At some point a world leader will receive power from an alien being known as the "dragon," identified in the Book of Revelation as Satan! John wrote in Revelation of the "beast" political system and its ruler, the Antichrist. The beast is not only the system; it is definitely "a man" (Rev. 13:16). We are told that the beast gets his power from the dragon, Satan, who could be viewed as an extraterrestrial being.

"And I stood upon the sand of the sea, and saw a beast rise up out of the sea, having seven heads and ten horns, and upon his horns ten crowns, and upon his heads the name of blasphemy. And the beast which I saw was like unto a leopard, and his feet were as the feet of a bear, and his mouth as the mouth of a lion: and *the dragon gave him his power, and his seat, and great authority"* (Rev. 13:1,2). That the dragon is Satan is established in the previous chapter of Revelation: "And the great dragon was cast out, that old serpent, called the Devil, and Satan, which deceiveth the whole world: he was cast out into the earth, and his angels were cast out with him...the accuser of our brethren is cast down, which accused them before our God day and night...Woe to the inhabiters of the earth and of the sea! for the devil is come down unto you, having great wrath, because he knoweth that he hath but a short time" (Rev. 12:9-12).

In recent months, people harassed by UFO occurrences have called us for personal counsel. Parents have reached out to us for answers to give to their teenagers, who are hearing things in school and on television that have raised questions about UFOs.

When the real, crushing necessity for this information becomes more apparent in time to come, you will have the means to provide the answers. When the last stage of the delusion begins, it will not come gradually. It will come crashing in around people of Earth. It will be appealing. The delusion will look like truth and will appeal to the flesh. It will offer solutions to all our major world problems and explanations for many mysteries.

This book could be a threat to the government, the apostate Church, the New Age movement, the international money brokers, the power brokers of Earth in general. Leaders in the New Age have already labeled people like us as "the bad seed" because we refuse to adapt to their "new reality." We want you to take this matter very seriously. Events in the near future will prove the worth of this work and the validity of our warnings. Mankind is ready now for the masterwork of deception that is in the wings, waiting to come on stage for the final conflict.

CHAPTER TWO

NINE GLEAMING DISKS

On June 24, 1947, Kenneth Arnold, a businessman from Boise, Idaho, was flying his light plane over Washington state. He spotted what he described as "nine gleaming disks" traveling at a fantastic rate of speed. They skimmed across the sky like quicksilver. What could they be? By timing the passage of the objects from one mountain peak to another, Arnold was able to estimate their speed at an incredible 1,700 miles per hour. Amazingly, they could make ninety-degree turns without slowing down! Later, when pressed for details by newspaper reporters, he said, "Well, they looked like flying saucers." Thus a term was coined and an era was born.

While there are ancient records of UFO sightings, the Kenneth Arnold incident marks the beginning of the great awareness of UFOs in modern times. Now the idea of UFOs and aliens from space has become an absolute fascination for mankind. What the world first looked upon with interested skepticism has become an increasingly accepted idea. Today the UFO phenomenon is sweeping the world. Children from their earliest years watch countless hours of space fantasy on television that is all too real to impressionable young minds.

Talk shows and books on the topic are hot items for ratings and sales. Motion pictures such as *2001, A Space Odyssey; E.T.; Close Encounters of the Third Kind; Star Wars;* and *Star Trek* break box office records. Television abounds with documentaries about the UFO phenomenon. It is no wonder that most Americans believe that UFOs are real. If UFOs are real, what does that reality imply? These films and documentary dramatizations not only entertain; there is an ominous side to the whole scheme. The menace is that they lure people into an alternative philosophy and world-view that stands in direct contradiction to the Christian faith as found in the Bible.

Accounts of close encounters with entities from other worlds can be read in newspapers and magazines almost daily. Strange experiences with beings from other realms of existence are reported in best-selling books such as *The Interrupted Journey,* which relates the UFO saga of Barney and Betty Hill and Whitley Strieber's books *Communion* and *Transformation.* Erich von Daniken's book *Chariots of the Gods* and others in the series have sold millions of copies in many languages. Brad Steiger and Ruth Montgomery are prominent New Age authors whose best-sellers appeal to a public looking for answers to one of the most incredible mysteries of all time — the mystery of UFOs.

Paul Harvey, a reliable mainline news commentator, who confesses to being an evangelical Christian, recently (January 21, 1991) reported sightings of a 350-foot elliptically-shaped object that hovered 500 feet off the ground over a military installation in Yugoslavia. Reportedly, it traveled 2,000 miles to be sighted again only four minutes later at a distant location. Television programs investigate and report on both past and current UFO sightings. "Hard Copy" reported sightings in Belgium, Italy, Spain, and Switzerland observed by many people simultaneously. "Unsolved Mysteries" has had ongoing reports about the unexplained circles appearing in wheat fields in the United Kingdom, the USSR, Canada, and the

U.S.A. Celebrities such as Shirley MacLaine and astronauts such as John Young, Gordon Cooper, and John Glenn claim to have had close encounters with alien beings.

RECENT EVENTS AS REPORTED ON NATIONAL TELEVISION

On May 17, 1991 a CBS television special, "Visitors From the Unknown — UFO Abductions," began with these words: "The following program will present ideas that may be contrary to your present beliefs. Tonight we will examine CLOSE ENCOUNTERS of the FOURTH KIND. Witnesses not only have had personal contact with extraterrestrial life forms, but were also detained by them. The recreations of aliens and their spacecraft are based upon a composite of testimonies and research."

The first testimonial was given by Travis Walton. On November 5, 1975, Travis was working with a logging crew in Arizona. He was abducted by a UFO, examined on board the craft, and later released. His fellow workers saw the incident and fled the scene in terror in a pickup truck. The police suspected that they had murdered Walton and had cooked up the UFO tale as an alibi. When Travis Walton reappeared, he confirmed the bizarre story.

Next, Alan Godfrey, a British police officer, claimed that on October 23, 1977, near West Yorkshire, England, he was abducted by aliens in a spacecraft. In each of these cases the space vehicles were described as elliptical (saucer) in shape. Godfrey also witnessed to having been physically examined and then released.

The third witness, John Salter and his twenty-three-year-old son, John Salter, III, were traveling from North Dakota on the way to Mississippi on a lecture tour. While traveling through southern Wisconsin on March 20, 1988, they met up with a UFO. Both men appeared on the CBS special and described seeing a UFO, meeting the aliens, and being carried away in the spacecraft. Again there was a physical examination, but Salter said that he liked the aliens and wished he could meet them again. The two first witnesses emphasized the terror they experienced throughout the ordeal.

The CBS television special concluded with this: "These have been but three of hundreds of reported UFO encounters. While no scientific proof is available to the public, one thing remains clear — a growing number of people believe extraterrestrial life exists, and still others believe Earth is being visited regularly. If so, where are they from? What do they want? These questions remain unanswered."

A local television station, Channel Three in Springfield, Missouri, featured a recent sighting in Tennessee where a circular depression in a grass field was evidence left behind indicating the presence of a UFO. Larry Thurmond took video pictures of a UFO in that area of Tennessee. His video clip was shown along with shots of the circle in the grass.

The newscaster on Channel Three summed it up with a question: "What do you think will be the total ramification of a real UFO contact here on Earth?"

Also in May, "Hard Copy," a network television magazine show, told the story of many UFO sightings in the Soviet Union. The program featured Dr. Marina Popovitch who is a retired Soviet Air Force colonel. She is also a test pilot with many world records to her credit. She is a scientist and Soviet UFO expert. "Hard Copy" showed many pictures of Soviet sightings verified by top Soviet Air Force generals and others.

"Hard Copy" described one sighting over Moscow that was seen by hundreds of Soviet military personnel and thousands of civilians. Dr. Marina Popovitch confirms that the Soviet Politburo informed that at their Malta Summit conference, Presidents George Bush and Mikhail Gorbachev discussed a UFO sighting by Russian scientists. It involved a Soviet space probe that had been sent to Mars. Dr. Popovitch described her personal sighting of a UFO, which was also seen by hundreds of other people.

The list of scientists, astronauts, politicians, clergymen,

homemakers, businesspeople, and people from all walks of life who have come out of the closet to admit to UFO sightings or actual alien contacts is growing daily. President Jimmy Carter claims to have seen a UFO that he believes to be from outer space. Our government spends millions to fund a major project for which the sole purpose is to search for evidence of beings from other worlds (SETI — Search for Extraterrestrial Intelligence). Is science fiction coming true? Are we being visited by benign beings? Or is it possible that Earth is being invaded by destructive agents from somewhere else?

STRANGE AND CHANGING TIMES

These events are important because the ideas they generate can affect a person's eternal destiny. This age will see the culmination of events set in motion at creation, at the very dawn of human history. Things the Bible foretold for the close of this age and the coming of the true kingdom of God on Earth are coming into plain view. We need to be informed of the "sure word of prophecy" revealed in the Bible. Also, we need to be keenly aware of how people understand major ideas and events of our times. People's perception of reality regulates their actions and behavior.

Right now our world is being hijacked by a deceptive philosophy promoted by entities beyond the normal realm of perception, but not beyond our realm of existence. These beings are not "aliens" in the "little green men from Mars" sense of the word. But they are alien to the purposes of God and His followers. They are ancient, evil foes of mankind and of God. They did not arrive on this planet in spaceships. They are not here to lead us into a New Age of Aquarius and world peace. They are here for deception and the final destruction of the race of man once and for all time. Now that even the secular world is taking note of the reality of demonic possession, it is time for us to reveal the true nature of these "visitors" among us.

We are asking some very important and fundamental questions. Who or what is God? Who and what is man?

From where did we originate? Where are we going? We are talking about origins and destiny. We are also dealing with the question of the potential relationship between the Creator and His creation. Is man fallen and in need of redemption? Or are we on an upward spiral of improvement that is about to receive major aid from the "ascended masters" of the "hierarchy of the universe?" These questions and the answers to them are at the very heart of the Bible.

This is a serious subject and must now be dealt with in a responsible fashion. In dealing with the mystery of UFOs, we are not on the lunatic fringe of theology. Instead, we stand on your behalf on the front line of battle. We are in defensive warfare at a major point of an assault on humanity. We are engaged in a "War of the Worlds," the world of Satan and his demonic hordes against the kingdom of God.

Here is an eight-point position statement that will help you understand this book. These points, which we believe we can prove to you, provide an understanding of the UFO phenomenon and how it affects our world today:

1. Whatever these objects are, they do exist. UFOs have a physical manifestation. UFOs and the beings that humans encounter through their experiences with them are real.

2. They are not from other planets. They are not spaceships that have traveled at warp-speed to visit our world. They have been here from the dawn of existence — in a spiritual dimension that is as real as the one we inhabit.

3. They are supernatural in nature. Rather than from the physical world, the UFOs are from the realm of the paranormal or the spiritual. This does not prevent them from having a material manifestation.

4. They are demonic. The current wave of UFOs is not from the realm of the angels of God. They are manifestations of evil spirits that serve Satan and his purposes. Abundant evidence will be offered to prove this point. The authors have not one reservation or doubt about this. We do not know of any evangelical, conservative Bible scholar or

theologian who has dealt with this question who disagrees with us.

5. The purpose of UFOs is deception. The entities behind UFOs are not merely poltergeists ("playful ghosts"). They have definite plans and purposes, and those plans do not auger well for mankind. Their principal weapon is deception. They are here to destroy us, but they can be defeated by ordinary people who are willing to undertake extraordinary measures.

6. They figure into the end-time scheme of prophecy and its fulfillment. The increasing frequency of sightings and "close encounters" are a part of an end-time assault on humanity. The prophecies of the Bible clearly reveal this. Both the seemingly benign and the hostile entities are playing their diverse roles.

7. They will play an increasing role in preparing a segment of humanity for the reception of the Antichrist.

8. Several of the Bible's end-time prophecies can now be more clearly understood when we consider the UFO delusion. For example, the UFO idea will provide one way for sinful humanity to explain away the rapture of the Church. Mankind will demand an explanation for the disappearance of 250 to 500 million people when the 1 Thessalonians 4:16-18 event occurs.

And we have the word of the prophets made more certain, and you will do well to pay attention to it, as to a light shining in a dark place, until the day dawns and the morning star rises in your hearts (2 Pet. 1:19; NIV).

CHAPTER THREE

THE ARKANSAS INCIDENT

On Friday, October 20, 1989, Joanne Wilson, a business-person from Harrison, Arkansas was involved in a bizarre UFO encounter. Joanne, an evangelical Christian and her business companion were observed, followed, and harassed by a UFO for almost an hour. Joanne suffered from strange dreams and nightmares, all directly connected to the incident. There were physical after effects. There may also be a problem of "lost time." The incident took place in the darkness of night, in the wee hours of the morning. What could be the meaning of this strange event and thousands of others like it? It is the opinion of this writer that the two women involved in the incident were set up by the deceivers, not only to be deceived, but to serve as a channel to bring subtle deception to humanity. We believe that by the grace of God the deceivers' plan was frustrated and will not see fulfillment here. Let this be a warning that further attempts will be made to break through this credibility barrier. The deceivers cannot tolerate the idea that a significant body of people refuse to accept the new reality. Events must be manipulated so it can be said, "Of course, born-again Christians have also had direct contact with the space brothers. They will testify that these are the very angels of

God sent to help us in these troubled times." Even hostile contacts with evangelicals would be desirable, as it would offer the desired evidence for the deceivers' case.

If Joanne could have been persuaded by the event, and subsequently through hypnotic regression to "remember" having direct contacts with aliens from space, it would help the cause of the deceivers. This could have been portrayed as the first time a born-again Christian had direct contact with an extraterrestrial. It would not shatter our basic premise, that the UFOs are paranormal and diabolical, but it would contradict one of our sub-premises. That sub premise is that, according to our observation and analysis, those who have had close encounters of the third kind have a predilection for the paranormal. The women involved in this incident have rejected hypnotic regression, though it has been strongly recommended to them by UFO researchers put in contact with them by NASA.

Chapters Three and Four present the first interview conducted with the two UFO witnesses in Harrison, Arkansas. The text has been legitimately edited only to delete voice substitutions, and to smooth out the grammar of the spoken word. It does not deviate, even slightly, from the sense of the interview. You will still note the informal conversational style.

The second woman involved seems to disagree with our premise, that UFOs are demonic. Perhaps she has not made up her mind yet. Out of courtesy to her, knowing her wishes in the matter, we will not use her name in this book. It should be noted, however, that her identity is a matter of public record through interviews she willingly granted to local and regional newspapers.

Here is the interview, conducted in the Wilson home:

David Lewis: I understand that you're a businessperson?

Joanne Wilson: Yes, I have an antique and gift shop. [She has since sold her shop and is now a real estate agent.]

D.L. Now getting right to the subject of what we're discussing here . . . what was the date of the occurrence, the

UFO incident?

J.W. It was October the 20th, on a Friday, early in the morning.

D.L. How early in the morning?

J.W. I got up at 4 A.M., and by the time I got to Jane Doe's [the other woman who traveled with her] house it was close to 5 A.M. So we left around 5.

D.L. Where were you going?

J.W. To War Eagle area. It's about three miles from the actual show where we went.

D.L. Now, where they have this War Eagle craft show — is that what it's called, War Eagle Craft Show?

J.W. Yes, it's out in the country. It's on War Eagle Creek.

D.L. Where were you when you first noticed the UFO?

J.W. It was the other side of Huntsville. I went back and retraced this, so I'd be sure. Just out of Huntsville, not very far, probably ten or twenty minutes, not farther than that. I didn't really get my mileage. We had gone through Huntsville, so it was the other side.

D.L. You're driving along and what happened?

J.W. We came around a curve. Of course we were talking. It was early morning, and the stars were out. It was a real clear, beautiful morning, but it was night. We came around a curve, and there was a mountain, you know a valley and a mountain back to my left, and there was a real white light up there. I don't know if this was part of it or not. And I said, "What is that bright light up there?" Then I thought, *Oh, it's probably a night light, or something like that, because there are lots of chicken houses in the area.*

D.L. Was it on ground level?

J.W. It was up on the mountain. I really couldn't see. I wasn't thinking that much about it, really. But when I retraced it one night when I went back to see our route, I looked for the light on the mountain, but the light was not there. So it could be part of this.

D.L. The mountain where you saw the light... when you

went back and retraced it, that was in the daytime?

J.W. No, it was at night too.

D.L. Have you ever been there — have you ever been through there during the daytime to see what it looked like?

J.W. Not lately. I need to go back.

D.L. You don't know whether there's a building there or not?

J.W. No, I don't. I'm not real sure what that light was, one way or the other. I just know I couldn't find it. I was really looking for that mountain with that light on it, and the light wasn't there, so it kind of confused me. But anyway, immediately after that, Jane said to me, of course we were still talking, you know, it was just all these things to catch up on, "What is that light?" And I didn't know what she was talking about. She saw it first.

D.L. Now who is she again?

J.W. I'll call her "Jane." (The other party involved wishes not to be identified in this book.)

D.L. And she's your partner in the craft business?

J.W. Yes, we work together in our craft show. We had a booth together. I looked over there, and it wasn't up in the sky now; it was straight out. I could look out through her window [the women were riding in a pickup that they used to haul their booth and materials] without looking up, it was just straight out there, and it was a big red glow. It was huge. It was as big as this kitchen, that long, and maybe wider and taller.

D.L. And this was to the right of the road?

J.W. This was to the right, this light was.

D.L. I want you to know that this does not have a ring of unreality to it.

J.W. Okay.

D.L. On three occasions I have observed similar sightings. That's why my interest has been sparked in this subject. I saw a UFO in 1952 in Kansas City, Missouri. It was seen by many people and was reported on the local radio stations. It was a large metallic object. It was daytime.

I saw a sighting in northern California. It was a nighttime sighting reported by many people. It's questionable whether it was a UFO or something else. One of my daughters has had a major UFO sighting. It was near St. Louis. I had another UFO sighting, which was seen by many people, including the county sheriff in Ephrata, Washington. That would have been back around — again I'd have to look up records, but I'm guessing around 1968.

So, having had this background, I've had a very intense interest in the subject. I've talked to a lot of people who have had these kinds of experiences. I know a lot of reliable, stable Christians who have had experiences of this nature. I wanted to explain my point of view up front so you would know that you are talking to a person who is sympathetic. I'm not sitting here as a skeptic, thinking you are some kind of a nut because of what you have seen.

J.W. We saw the light out to the right, this big red-orange glow. It was huge. It was up off the ground. It did not touch the ground, and it was not in the sky. It was just out there.

And she would say, "What is this light?"

I looked at it, and I said, "I don't know."

And she'd say, "What's this light?"

I'd say, "I don't know."

This was our conversation for a few minutes. You know, "What's the light? I don't know." And I kept thinking, *What could this be?*

D.L. And it was moving along on the same plane as you were?

J.W. It was going at the same pace, yes, just right along with us.

D.L. Roughly, how far do you think you were away from it?

J.W. I had guessed it to be at least within a hundred feet. I'd say a hundred feet.

D.L. That close?

J.W. There was a ditch and a fence, and then it was just right out there in the field. And I try to think of the distance like the length of a house, you know, a hundred-foot-long house, or something. I might be wrong; at night it's hard to estimate.

D.L. And the size of the object you would guess to be....

J.W. It was large. It was at least as big as this room. I think it's twenty-four feet.

D.L. Did it have any definable form? Or, was it like a cloud of gas?

J.W. It was like a cloud of gas or fog or something like that. Very dense though. But the light did not shine out. It didn't light the trees or the ground or anything. It was all contained within itself.

D.L. Was it bright or dull or what?

J.W. It was fairly bright, but it wasn't so bright that you couldn't look at it.

D.L. Well, that is interesting. Did it always stay the same size?

J.W. At times it would fade, or it would get brighter. And also, the sides would either get larger or smaller. It didn't stay the same.

D.L. Okay.

J.W. But most of the time it stayed pretty large. So we kept going along, and I was thinking, *Could this be a balloon? Could it be fog? Could it be a cloud?* All these things came to my mind. But my mind would not answer. There just was no answer for it. And then there were big columns of light. They were white, white lights that came on inside it. They were so far from the bottom and so far from the top. They didn't touch the top or the bottom.

D.L. Columns of light inside the cloud of light?

J.W. Columns of light, inside the red glow. Right. Two big white columns came on. I thought, *Well, this is really happening. This is the real thing.* Then you really panic. And one of them, the one on the right, would sometimes go like a windshield wiper, very slow, back and forth. And then the lights, the columns of light would disappear at times.

D.L. Did you at any point stop the car and look at it?

J.W. Yes, we did. Jane grabbed her camera and started taking pictures. And I thought, *Those will not take. It's a little bitty 110. There is no way those pictures will take.* But I said, "Let's stop. If you're going to take pictures, let's stop and get some good shots." Now I think, *Why did we do it?* But we stopped. I've got power windows on the truck, and I put the window down on Jane's side. We had the doors locked, and we had the window down. She took a couple of pictures there, and that's the two that turned out. And when we took the pictures, it dissolved, almost completely. It just dissolved itself. I thought to myself, *Whatever it is doesn't want its picture made.*

D.L. There's intelligence involved here.

J.W. Yes, there was. There was something. Because when we stopped to take the pictures, it stopped. It didn't go on. It stopped with us.

D.L. So, in other words, this object was identifying with you and your motion through time and space. Let me be sure about that — it was definitely moving with you? This was not a haphazard thing?

J.W. No. It was definitely — you know, exactly out from us. Not behind, or in front, just exactly out beside us. When we stopped to take the pictures, it stopped. When we took them, it kind of dissolved itself. And I thought, *Well, it's going away.* So we wheeled — I got real scared at that point. Something about it was really terrifying. We pulled back on the highway, and it started again. It showed up real bright and went right with us, and it went all the way. We missed our turn, of course, and we even got hysterical. We got to laughing, I think to keep from really cracking up. But we got to laughing about it, and she was laughing, and tears were rolling down her eyes. Jane said, "I bet I've got black under my eyes." As if it really mattered.

I thought, *There's no answer for this. I don't know what it is.*

When the lights first came on, Jane said, "What are we going to do?"

I said, "Well, there's nothing we can do."

I said within myself, *God will just have to take care of us.* Then I said it out loud: "God will have to take care of us." We were pretty scared. We just didn't know what to think.

D.L. If you were afraid and thought, "God will have to take care of us," it was obvious to you that this thing was not benevolent nor did it have good intentions. It was something that inspired fear. I want to understand this clearly. Is it correct that at that point of time you had no thought that the thing might be there for any good reason? Instead your response was one of fear and to call on God for His aid?

J.W. That's right. At the time, I really thought it was beings from some other planet.

D.L. We've been conditioned to think that. Television, the print media and a host of books have projected this concept.

J.W. Yes, that's right. But it was not anything of God. It was not sent from God. I knew that. There was fear. Of course, fear of the unknown ....

D.L. Being a Christian, without a lot of background information, you knew that this was evil and not something sent from God. Various Christian authors have written about UFOs, but I guess you were not aware of that at the time. I get the feeling that you instinctively knew that this was not something sent from God.

J.W. It was not. No way was it from God.

D.L. You're absolutely right, and on a much deeper level than you could even imagine. But we will discuss that.

J.W. I want to add a few things. Of course we missed our road, Route 303. We were so shook up and scared. But you know, right after this, we talked about it and we said, "Well we really weren't scared," but we were. I don't know why we thought we weren't, but we were. When I think back about it, we were terrified. So we missed our road and this is the strange thing. There were a lot of places to turn around. It's probably fifteen miles from 303 to Springdale. We could have turned around, but we didn't. We went all the way to Springdale. We both remember the sign that said, "Springdale City Limits."

There was a point when we didn't see the light. We couldn't see it. And I said, "Jane, I have got to stop a minute."

And about that time she said, "It's overhead, it's over us." And she took a couple of pictures there that didn't turn out because she took them through the windshield. I stopped anyway, just for a minute, and this is on the left as we're going back the other way now. Then the light came over the truck, and it came over to my side, and it lit up very brightly. Not to hurt your eyes, but it was very bright, and the columns of light came back on.

D.L. Were you driving the pickup?

J.W. Right. See, it would actually have been on the same side it was before, but we were going the other way.

D.L. Oh, I see, you had turned around?

J.W. We had turned around and started back and had stopped by a trailer house, so then it was on my side. I said, "Jane, go ahead and take a picture. It's really brightened up for us, take a picture, now." Well, those didn't take. And so we pulled out on the road...

D.L. Why do you suppose they didn't take?

J.W. The red lights. It's my theory. I think the red lights covered ... whatever.

D.L. But the white light was there visible to your eyes? Whatever is visible to your eyes, physically, should show up on the picture.

J.W. Should photograph? I've got one with a streak of light, but it doesn't really look like the columns. But this one...

D.L. You've got to understand; this is not an uncommon thing.

J.W. Is that right?

D.L. For pictures to be blurred or to come out non-existent, even when conditions were right. Now, that sort of indicates something very interesting, that we're dealing with paranormal or spiritual phenomenon. We're dealing with something that's supernatural.

J.W. We sat and looked at it. We had the window down, and I just sat there. That was the first time I had the chance to really see it. I was trying to drive during all this other part. So I sat there and just looked at it for a little while, and it just stayed there real bright. Those columns of light, one was moving. Then we pulled back on the road and it went with us. We turned on 303, and it went with us, turned with us, stayed with us, until we were almost to our destination. We were just ready to turn in our driveway at the craft show, and it disappeared. And the way it disappeared. Jane didn't even see it disappear, but I did. It was so fast. I mean, you'd have to really — you barely catch it. You almost think, *Did I see that, or did I not see that?* But this red light just came together, and when it did, it made a crashing sound.

D.L. You heard it?

J.W. Yes, I heard that. At that point I heard it. Before it was definitely silent. As a matter of fact, everything was silent. It was a real quiet...

D.L. The crashing sounded like something heavy, but it dropped? Like a transformer on a telephone pole exploding because it's been hit by lightning, or...?

J.W. Mmmmm, well, not really. I can't explain it. It's kind of a crashing thump, and the crackling sound with it.

D.L. The crackling sound gives it the . . . the impression of something energetic or electrical?

J.W. Yes. Something like that. Jane didn't hear it. I heard it. And when it came together, this red light just came together and made that sound, and right down the middle was the black, kind of like just a streak, crooked, kind of like lightning, when it came together. And that was it, it was gone. It had stayed with us up to that point. Now from the time that we saw it — well, let's go back, from 303 to Springdale is probably fifteen miles. There and back is thirty miles. I think we were driving about fifty or fifty-five. And then our turn to the show was probably five miles. So see there's thirty-five miles, and we saw it on down the road before we ever got to 303. So it was thirty-five to forty miles it followed us.

J.W. That's a long time, believe me. But a little less maybe. At the time it did not seem that long. We talked about it yesterday, and I said, "I went up and redrove that route. And from where we turned around at Springdale, back to that trailer is a long way." I asked her, "How do you remember that?"

She said, "Well, I thought we just pulled out on the road for a minute and then pulled into the trailer."

I said, "That's what I thought. I thought it was just right down from the store." But it's not. It's quite a little distance there. So that's kind of confusing.

D.L. Yes. Time can get distorted, though, when you're observing something that's completely out of the ordinary. You were a little shaky at this point?

J.W. I didn't really shake over it. It was just — we were quiet.

D.L. When I said shaky, I didn't mean that physically. I meant were you feeling emotionally shook up?

J.W. Yes, I was shook up inside. And Jane was too because she was running around in the little booth there, saying, "I can't do this. I just can't put these things up. I don't know where to put it. You're just going to have to do it, I can't." And she was just going around in circles. And I am used to having help...

D.L. I understand. Did she seem disoriented?

J.W. Yeah, she was. She was just kind of running around. And I guess I was more calm because I have a shop, and I'm used to doing things like that. So, to me, it came automatically. I was just putting it up without really thinking.

D.L. You were going through the motions, without allowing the whole experience to dictate a change of your normal physical pattern of activity?

J.W. I was just going ahead. And I remember, I felt very hot. It was cold that morning. I don't know what the temperature was, but I was thinking I should go back and check the temperature in the paper that morning. But it was cold.

D.L. What do you think that means?

J.W. We had layered ourselves with clothes because we knew it was going to be a cold day. We didn't have our coats on; they were in the truck. First of all, we got our coats out, and I was putting my coat on, and I said, "I can't stand this coat; I'm too hot." You know, I was just burning up.

D.L. Like you had a fever?

J.W. Yeah, like a fever, and my face just felt hot. It was like it was going to explode. Have you ever been in a room where it felt like the temperature was a hundred, and you had on wool, and you just thought you were going to die if you didn't get out of that room? And you just felt hot? That's how it was, till probably noon. And I said, "I think I'm going to have to go get some of these layers of clothes off; I'm burning up." Well, she wasn't hot, but she was just running around, saying, "I'm cold. I've got to get this heater hooked up; we're going to freeze." We were opposite. And we were very quiet. You'd think when something like that happened, you'd be asking people, "Did you see this?" Or, "Did you see this light?" We didn't ask anybody. We didn't tell anybody all day. Every once in awhile we'd mention to each other, "What was that we saw?" And that's, you know, about it. But we were very quiet. We got home that night and told our husbands. Then she called everybody. I didn't tell anybody, really. I just didn't want to talk to anyone about it. But Jane did.

CHAPTER FOUR

THE AFTERMATH

D.L. How did people react initially to what she had to say?

J.W. Everybody believed it. Everybody really believed it. I didn't think they would.

D.L. Well possibly, it's because you're a believable person.

J.W. I suppose. But everybody has believed it, and you would not believe the phone calls and the people that have come out to see the pictures. I finally just left them at the shop because everybody wanted to see them. But the surprising thing is that they say, "What do you think this is?"

Well, I didn't really know. I hadn't studied this. I had no idea, really, except from what you heard, beings from outer space, or I'd heard it could be demonic. Well, I had decided before this happened that they probably were demonic. And that was what was in my mind. But then, when I saw it, I thought, "No, these are actually beings." So, when they would ask me that question, I would say, "I do not know. There could be beings, or it could be demonic."

And you know, most people would say, "What do you mean? What is that?"

And I'd say, "Well, demons."

And they'd say, "What's that?"

That surprised me. That really surprised me.

D.L. You'd have a hard time getting that idea across to an average, non-religious person, and to a certain extent, even to some religious persons. Most people in Christian circles, except the Pentecostals and Charismatics, have very little consciousness of any supernatural type of activity.

J.W. I tried to tell them. But, of course, they didn't understand. But there were a few people, and I think you're right, it was the born-again Christian people that would understand. But most of the people do not know what a demon is. I was surprised. The first person that we actually told was Jane's husband because we came back to her house first. Then my husband came over because we were late getting back. He thought maybe something had happened, so he came to check on us.

D.L. Is your husband a believer?

J.W. My husband is a believer, a born-again Christian.

D.L. When you told him about the experience, what was his initial reaction?

J.W. We said, "Well, we saw a light." Of course, all we had was just our story.

And he said, "Oh, it was probably, you know, something else."

And I said, "No, I don't think so."

D.L. It did seem to manifest intelligence. Because when you tried to take pictures, there was a fading. There was a starting, there was a stopping, there was a following, there was an identification between your motion and the motion of it.

J.W. That's right. Definitely. Because I knew when we were going along, I thought, *There's something that is maneuvering that.* It's controlled by someone. And I think that was what caused me to fear. What is it? What is out there? What will happen next? What am I going to see next?

D.L. Dr. J. Allen Hynek was one of the greatest UFO researchers from a non-religious, strictly scientific standpoint of view. He was a credible scientist involved with Project Blue Book for the United States Air Force. That was one of the biggest investigations on UFOs that was ever done. Officially, Project Blue Book was closed. But, unofficially, the investigation has never stopped. It's an ongoing investigation.

Most airline pilots who see a UFO won't report it. The reason for that is because if they report it, they will go through hours and hours of debriefing and interrogation. Some claim that they almost felt like they were being treated like criminals. The degree to which they grill them is unbelievable. So, the reporting of UFOs from a lot of sources, in the military, and in the flight industry, has fallen off dramatically because people have gotten the word that if you report this type of thing, you're going to have to go through a whole process that could be rather unpleasant.

The thing about Dr. Hynek that interests me is the fact that he arrived at a conclusion similar to my own. That is, that UFOs have a paranormal origin. The difference is that I arrive at my conclusion as a theologian, as a Bible scholar, whereas he arrives at it purely as a physical scientist. In many ways Hynek expressed his opinion that there is something supernatural or even occultic about the UFO phenomenon. He talks about gods from outer space and the legends of the gods; that's the von Daniken theory. Are you at all familiar with that name?

J.W. The legends of the gods? Well, you talked about it on your tape.

D.L. Gods from outer space and so on. Here it is again, a linkage with the occult. And you can just scan through this book. And here this author talks about the Pascagoula UFO abduction case in Mississippi, and then there is the Barney and Betty Hill case. Barney and Betty were allegedly abducted by a UFO while driving. They awakened in their vehicle and noted that a span of time had passed of which they were not conscious. Later, under hypnotic regression they recalled being on the UFO and being medically examined. Later Barney died and Betty believes it was a result of the examination. Sounds unbelievable, but a number of scientists were convinced. I have studied many of these cases. I have read a lot of transcripts. I have read hundreds of books and articles on the subject. The interesting thing about Dr. Hynek's views is that he believes that the solution to the mystery may lie in the parapsychological realm. The report from Iron Mountain deals with this, and that's a very strange one indeed. Hynek said, for example, there's just too much nuts and bolts evidence to deny that the UFOs have a material, physical manifestation. But he said on various occasions that he didn't really think that they came from other planets but rather from a psychic source or maybe from a parallel realm. This is exactly the conclusion that I had arrived at in 1952 when I began my own research. They're either angelic or they're demonic, if I'm correct, and if Hynek is correct. Hynek, of course, would add a third category. Or he could waive my two categories, demons and angels, aside and simply say that they are beings in another dimension.

Look at this quotation about Hynek: "Dr. Hynek's attitude on the origin of UFOs has changed over the years ... From arch-debunker to an advocate of the interplanetary hypothesis, he now leans toward a psychic explanation." And, look at this quotation from J. Allen Hynek:

"I would have to say that the extraterrestrial theory is a naive one. It's the simplest of all hypotheses, but not a very likely explanation for the phenomenon we have seen manifesting itself over centuries. In Toronto, Canada, not too long ago, I spoke before a group of liberal-thinking scientists who had gathered for a serious discussion on the latest discoveries in the field of parapsychology. The conference was sponsored by the New Horizons Research Foundation that is ably presided over by Dr. George Owen, a former fellow of Trinity College, Cambridge, England. I told these astute men of learning — including a respected Nobel Prize winner in physics — that we should consider the various factors that strongly suggest a linkage, or at least a parallelism, with the occurrences of a paranormal nature. Among the factors that belie the interplanetary theory is the proneness of certain individuals to have repeated UFO experiences. Another peculiarity is the alleged ability of certain UFOs to dematerialize. A plasma is said to envelope the object in many cases. Then the 'cloud' becomes more and more opaque until it completely obscures the UFO. Finally the whole cloud vanishes as though going into another dimension ... these are the types of psychic phenomena that are confronting us in the UFO mystery."

Joanne, that has a certain similarity to your experience. Also it is interesting that what showed up on the pictures was different from what you observed.

I believe that if one takes a biblical standpoint of view, the conclusion is that they are either angels or demons. My conclusion is that they are demonic. Why is it the world can believe in supernatural phenomena and supernatural beings but reject the biblical teaching on evil spirits?

If one wants to get an overview of the subject from a nonbiblical perspective, an interesting book to read is *The Aquarian Revelations* by Brad Steiger. He traveled all over the country, interviewing hundreds of people who claimed to have had actual contact with alien beings from UFOs. The essential "message" that comes from this type of interview is that we're about to destroy ourselves on planet Earth. The ascended masters of the hierarchy of the universe are now in communication with certain people on this planet. They will select a human person and endow him with supernormal powers and knowledge. This man will lead us to world government and world peace.

I went to a New Age prayer meeting as an observer. Dr. Robert Muller, who for many years was the Assistant Secretary General of the United Nations, was one of the main speakers. Muller has resigned the UN post and is a major guru in the New Age movement. Muller talks about a second coming of a Christ that clearly is not Jesus. We are about to be offered membership in a galactic council. They will help us solve our problems of hunger, pollution, war, violence, and so forth.

Joanne, I find nothing in any of the UFO reports that glorifies Jesus Christ or that magnifies God as God is described to us in the Bible. There is some talk about god in UFO circles, but it's the god that you find by descending into your own consciousness, by meditation, or some other occultic technique. By doing this, you discover your own divine godhood, and you become "christed." Right now, literally, tens of thousands of Americans are becoming demon possessed because they're opening themselves to these extraterrestrial beings through the teachings of people like Ruth Montgomery.

J.W. It's strange you mentioned her. I checked some books out of the library, and that's one of the books that I got.

D.L. *Aliens Among Us?*

J.W. Yes, *Aliens Among Us*. And another book I checked out was *Situation Red*. It has documented cases, and I think it's okay. And then I got into Montgomery's book. I had just gotten various books on UFOs. I went ahead and read most of it because it gave me an insight into what they believe.

D.L. Well, Ruth Montgomery is at the leading edge of this teaching. What she's saying is that these beings are on Earth, in a spiritual form, and that if you'll open yourself to them, they will come into you. They will take over the processes of your life and intertwine their personality with your personality. They will help you solve your problems, and then you'll become a problem-solver to people around you. These beings that come into people are called "walk-ins" by Ruth Montgomery.

J.W. Spirit guides is another term. In the book, she's constantly talking to her spirit guide and telling what it said. I began to see because it would talk about people from other planets and how they're going to come here and rescue you, and all that.

D.L. By the way, Ruth Montgomery was the person who

popularized Jeanne Dixon by writing her first biography.

J.W. I have the book by Montgomery in there. I haven't taken it back yet.

D.L. There are a number of books in this series. There must be three or four in this series, and there will no doubt be more.

J.W. As a matter of fact, her book was so — it's so far out on the things they believe, I don't know how even the New Age followers could believe it. It's so twisted.

D.L. There is a depth of delusion in the world today that defies logic. Now, when were you first contacted by the press?

J.W. Jane got on the phone immediately. She called NASA. They gave her a number of a UFO research center.

D.L. Was it MUFON?

J.W. I'm not sure. She's got the address. I didn't even pay attention to it. But it's out of Illinois.

The two guys they sent to interview us were from Arkansas, but I wasn't impressed with them. In fact, you know, at a time when you're looking for answers ... Wait a minute. I left the newspaper clippings in the car.

[Joanne goes out to the car to get the news article.]

Here's the clipping from the Harrison paper; it should have the name in it.

D.L. What about this drawing in the newspaper?

J.W. The drawing has nothing to do with anything that we...

D.L. You mean the picture is just purely newspaper hype?

J.W. Yes, to get attention I think.

D.L. Let's look at this clipping. I thought I remembered seeing "UFO Network ... Mutual UFO Network." That's MUFON, that's the one ... When she contacted NASA, no one direct from NASA came?

J.W. No, they didn't. They referred her to this number, and she called.

D.L. I think these people will give all of this information to NASA. At NASA there are people who are total believers, and there are some who are totally skeptical.

J.W. These men were totally believers that there are beings from other planets. That's what they really want to believe.

D.L. Do you think people from the Mutual UFO Network, from MUFON, will tend to be completely believers in life from outer space?

J.W. That's right.

D.L. Now let's look at this from a biblical standpoint, just for a quick overview. Let's look at some facts. We know there are angelic beings. We know that on occasions these angels of God did materialize bodies and also physical objects for their use, like clothing, staffs, food, and so forth. If the demons are fallen angels, which is the most likely explanation for their existence, it would stand to reason that they also can, for their purposes, materialize physical objects and even what would appear to be alien life forms. I don't have any problem with that, especially when I read the Book of Revelation. The ninth chapter talks about some of the strange creatures that are going to be appearing on Earth during the time of the Tribulation, when there is going to be a releasing of the demonic hordes. In Chapter Sixteen it speaks of three alien beings who go forth to deceive the rulers of the Earth. [The three aliens in Revelation sixteen have an amphibian or reptilian appearance. Here is the reference. It was not read on the interview tape.]

> *And I saw three unclean spirits like frogs come out of the mouth of the dragon, and out of the mouth of the beast, and out of the mouth of the false prophet. For they are the spirits of devils, working miracles, which go forth unto the kings of the earth and of the whole world, to gather them to the battle of that great day of God Almighty* (Rev. 16:13,14).

When the three evil spirits go out, they will appear as aliens from another place (planet). So here in Revelation we read about three frog-like unclean spirits (demons).

They are not actually frogs, but "like" frogs. Probably that describes their alien features or appearance. They do go out as real, living creatures, as intelligent beings, to deceive the rulers of the Earth.

Joanne, I think the human race is being set up for this. Now what is happening here in Arkansas could have a real significance, and you are a major figure in this situation. The reason I feel this way is that with the exception of the Andreasson affair, there has never been a born-again Christian, to my knowledge, who had a close encounter of the third kind — an actual contact with alien beings.

What follows in the next three paragraphs was not a part of the interview. It has been added to explain the Andreasson case.

Both Betty Andreasson and her daughter Becky underwent extensive hypnotic regression to recover "lost memories." She remembered the aliens coming into her house and talking with them. Although reluctant, when the "alien" repeatedly asked her, "Will you follow us," Betty finally said, "Yes." We think that was a mistake. We hope that this book will serve as a warning to Christians not to have anything to do with aliens. We have tried to locate Betty or Becky Andreasson and find out more about their background and their present situation. We would like to know of the after effects of the hypnotherapy. So far we have been unable to locate them.

Their story is told in the book *The Andreasson Affair* by Raymond E. Fowler. Dr. J. Allen Hynek wrote the introduction of the book. In it he says, "The man on the street's simple opinion that either UFOs are all nonsense or that visitors from outer space do exist is brutally destroyed by close study ... The Andreasson case involves ... contactees, abduction, mental telepathy, mystical symbolism, and physical examination by 'aliens' ... and I now realize that it is a composite of many 'inputs...' Fowler is to be complimented on his perseverance in the investigation of this case of high 'strangeness...' The present work will also challenge those who consider UFOs solely synonymous with physical craft that transport flesh-and-blood denizens from distant solar systems ... here we have 'creatures of light' who find walls no obstacle to free passage into rooms and who find no difficulty in exerting uncanny control over witnesses' minds."[1]

Note the reference to "creatures of light" and the supernatural ability to walk through solid objects!

The interview with Joanne Wilson continues:

D.L. Many Christians have reported close encounters of the first kind. That's merely a sighting of a UFO. I've talked to some Christians who have seen physical evidence that UFOs had been present, like circles burnt in the earth. This would be a close encounter of the second kind. I investigated a case up in Smoky Lake, Alberta, Canada, on a CE-2. In your case a face-to-face confrontation with an alien did not take place. But did you have any dreams after this?

J.W. At first I had nightmares, but I couldn't remember them. I'd just wake up frightened. And then I had this one nightmare that I still remember vividly. In the dream it seemed like I was in a room, probably half the size of this room or a little bit bigger. And the walls were like a parachute, that kind of material, sort of. They were a grayish beige color, kind of a strange color. But the walls seemed to kind of be puffy. I thought I was standing here. This room also opened into another room. I couldn't see into the other room, but I was standing, say right here. And there was a — at the time I thought it was a coffin, that's what I thought it was — a coffin. It could have been a box or whatever. There was a person or some being laying in it. It was a man. He had on trousers and a shirt. I don't remember any shoes. And his clothes were the same color as the walls, that funny color. I thought he was very, very, very old — but like I told Mary, he had these really nice eyes. Well, they really were kind of like the people in India; you know, the pretty eyes that they have? He had beautiful eyes.

D.L. How were they shaped?

J.W. Kind of like people in India, just kind of, you know — pretty eyes. But they were too big for his face. They were like they didn't belong to him.

D.L. Have you seen the series of paintings of children with huge sad eyes? Was it anything like that?

J.W. Right, those big eyes, those big brown eyes. But he was very old. And I kept thinking, *Those eyes don't go with him; they don't match him. You know, the eyes are too nice for him because he doesn't look like that.*

D.L. Did he have normal features otherwise? Did he have a nose and a mouth?

J.W. I don't remember a nose. He had a mouth. I don't remember a nose or ears or hair. And his feet were kind of — you know, he didn't have any shoes. And they were kind of crossed or kind of laying together like that, and it seemed like his feet were kind of...

D.L. Was his head proportionate to his body or was it large or...

J.W. Pretty much so. And he had his hands — instead of having them, you know, like you do in a casket — I was thinking that in my dream. They're not like a person should be in a casket. He was laying there very still, but his fingers were like this. And I thought, *That's unusual because they should be lying down.* And I remember thinking, *His fingers are so long. They look like the beings in the space ship, without the hands...*

D.L. Let's back up on that. This may be important. Why did you have a memory of beings in the space ship? Because when you saw the light and the columns, you didn't see any beings, did you?

J.W. No.

D.L. But in the dream you were thinking that.

J.W. Right. But see, it could have had to do with one of these pictures. It looks like a hand in this picture [shows one of the photos Jane took], and I thought a lot about that hand. So it could have caused me to dream something like that. I don't know that it was, but it's a possibility. And he was — anyway this person or this being was staring at me, just intensely staring at me. He wouldn't take his eyes off of me. He just kept looking straight into my eyes. That was the only part of him that seemed alive. The rest of him just seemed like he was dead. It was a stare that said that he really did like me. He just really did like me. Like you know, a grandfather. I was telling Mary, like a grandfather would look at his grandchild with admiration, and just — I mean he just really did like me. But I didn't like him that well. I remember that if I would move a little his head moved, followed me ... His head was the only part that moved, just his head, kind of like a puppet, like that [Joanne motions with her own head.] It was real spooky. And when he did, he smiled. He had a big, wide mouth but he didn't have any teeth. His gums were real bloody red. And that's when I woke up.

D.L. There were no words?

J.W. No words.

D.L. No other creatures approached you in the dream?

J.W. They didn't approach me, or I wasn't concerned about them. It seemed like behind me, over here were some smaller creatures. But they were looking towards this other room. Their attention was focused on this doorway that led to the other room.

D.L. Not focused on the person in the box?

J.W. No and not on me. I really didn't pay attention to them. I just remember there were some over there, maybe four or five.

D.L. But in the dream you underwent no physical examination or no communication took place?

J.W. No.

D.L. Did the people from MUFON suggest hypnotic regression?

J.W. They suggested it. They didn't insist on it. They just said, "You can do it if you wish to." I thought they'd be real pushy about that.

D.L. Didn't it say in the paper that you talked to a psychiatrist?

J.W. The paper — no, I haven't. I don't think it said that.

But it did say that we were — it made it sound like we were real anxious to be hypnotized, and that's not true.

D.L. I forgot what the paper said. It does quote a doctor there who says, "Well, I'm no expert on this subject..." But who was that? I'm not recalling exactly what was in the clipping.

J.W. The Johnsons sighted [also saw] it in the woods. There was a doctor who did say something. Dr. Lynn Keener was bow hunting at 4:50 A.M. Friday, and he saw an orange light on the horizon. [Here Joanne has gotten the clipping from the *Harrison Daily Times* and is referring to it.]

D.L. Was he seeing the same area that you were?

J.W. It was the same area.

D.L. So I assume that he saw the same light. So there's a corroboration there?

J.W. Yes. But his light evidently did not move; it stayed in one spot.

D.L. This doctor — what kind of a doctor is he?

J.W. He's a dentist. He and his brother both are dentists.

D.L. When they suggested to you hypnotic regression, did they tell you the name of a doctor that you could see or a hypnotist?

J.W. Of course. They suggested a lady in Huntsville who had worked with them before on different cases.

D.L. How do you react to that possibility?

J.W. Well, it's just like I told them. I said, "I have never even thought about hypnosis. I know nothing about it. It's new to me. People have always told me it was — I don't know if I told them this, but people have always told me it was demonic and it's on the dark side, so I really just had placed it there and left it. And then when this came up, in my mind I began to think, *Well, you know, there is a possibility.* You're looking for answers. I thought, *Well, you know,* and I even got a book on that. I went to the library and got the book and read it, but I'm still not convinced.

D.L. Did you read about the Barney and Betty Hill case?

J.W. I haven't. I couldn't find the book; I'd asked for it.

D.L. We have that if you want to read it. Joanne, what I feel is happening is this:I believe that you were subjected to a demonic apparition, or you saw — not subjected to, but you saw a demonic apparition. I believe that the dreams were projected into your mind to create a scenario that would make an acceptance of alien beings palatable or thinkable in your mind. If you go into hypnotic regression now, you will not experience actual memories. It will be an implantation of false memories.

J.W. I had thought about that.

D.L. Under hypnosis you will seem to remember things that never really happened. You could remember being physically examined. You mentioned having a flushed feeling. Was there any change in the color of your skin?

J.W. Yes, I looked like I had been sunburned. [Subsequent interviews brought out more about physical effects, such as "burned" circles on thighs.]

J.W. And I had this rash. Of course, I have a rash a lot anyway. So I thought, *Well, it could just be normal,* but it was a little more than normal, and it's finally just about gone away.

But my face was red, and everybody commented, and my eyes.

D.L. Under hypnotic regression, it's possible that the idea could even be implanted that you had a liaison with these alien beings. What I'm describing here are things that have happened to other people, in quite a number of cases. I have interviewed people who underwent things of this nature prior to their accepting Christ. And they bought the whole story, you know? But, once they found Jesus Christ as Saviour, they realized that what they were under was a demonic delusion and what had taken place was demonic hypnosis.

I don't necessarily say that all hypnosis is demonic. But personally, for no reason would I ever subject myself to hypnosis. To be hypnotized successfully, you have to yield your will to another person. If that person, for any reason, doesn't have your best interest at heart or is inept or unskilled, or if there is a moment of carelessness, disaster could result. Under hypnosis you're in a state where you have yielded your will, and any kind of force or entity could conceivably enter into the situation. So, I would be very, very opposed to this. My advice to you would be not to accept hypnotic regression. The case of Bridy Murphy is one of the most famous cases of hypnotic regression. She was allegedly guided back into previous reincarnations by a hypnotist named Morrey Burnstein. Bridy Murphy was a false name. The book appeared back in the early fifties, and it made a big splash. Her real name was Jean Simmons. She was a homemaker who lived in Colorado. In her previous reincarnation her name was supposed to have been Bridget Murphy, who lived in Cork County, Ireland. She had memories of things that only someone very skilled in history would know about Cork County, Ireland. But that is not surprising because after all, Satan is aware of every aspect of everything that's ever happened in the world. I'm sure he has the most complete history books other than God himself, as far as that is concerned.

J.W. I had thought about that, just lately. The more I thought about it, I'd think, *Well, maybe I should do it; maybe I shouldn't do it.* I mean, you weigh this around because I'd never thought on it before, and it's all new to me. Lately I had thought, *Well, how do you know if it's you speaking, or someone else speaking?* It's not necessarily your answers. So I'm not going to do it [undergo hypnosis.]

D.L. Joanne, I'm going to have prayer with you today. If these MUFON people had succeeded in getting you into hypnotic regression, that would be a major breakthrough, and I'll tell you why. It would be the first time, as far as I know, that an evangelical Christian would be saying, "I have had a face to face encounter with an alien and I know they are real." If they could implant that within you, or if some demonic force could implant it within you, it would be horrible. You understand that being an object of this kind of attention is not a comfortable thing, as you have expressed to me in several ways.

J.W. No, it's not.

D.L. You've got to go around saying, "Oh, God, why me?"

J.W. I have. I thought, *Why would this happen to me? If it's of the devil, am I that evil and I don't know it that I attract him?"*

D.L. Probably the opposite is true. I think it's because you're a fine, stable Christian who is a respected church member. Not fanatical. So, in other words, you're a good middle of the roader. I talked to your pastor. This is the impression he gave me of you.

You're a businessperson, you've got an image of reliability. You're the most likely type of person for this kind of thing. You're the perfect model, in other words; you are desired because you would project credibility. If Satan could manipulate you now and use you for his purposes, he would advance his purposes greatly. Now, if Satan's purposes can be foiled in your life, then we have dealt a major blow to the kingdom of darkness, and he's going to have to find another candidate. Probably we can use your experience and example as a warning to others. It can be a warning to other Christians to be on the lookout.

J.W. People need to know. They absolutely need to know.

D.L. People need to know. Unfortunately there are, in our churches, vast areas of ignorance of things going on in our world today that are so important. Mary and Dell [people who introduced David Lewis to Joanne Wilson] can tell you that Ramona, my wife, and I work out there on the front lines, taking a stand for the Church on vital issues and concepts. And I thank God that the Church is tolerating me because I'm always out on the leading edge. Think of this — when I was sounding a warning about this very thing back in the mid-1950s, people must have thought I was off the wall. Well, nobody is thinking that now. People are waking up. Too much has happened and awareness is rising.

A United States naval commander came to me — this was quite some time ago. He was involved in a very frightening UFO experience. I can't go into detail without destroying a confidence. But suffice to say, I counseled this man, had prayer with him. So, Joanne, you can see that my background in this matter goes back — from 1952 to the present. As the Ramseys know, we're involved in research in a lot of different areas that some in the Church would really like to ignore because it's very uncomfortable. It is too demanding. One is thrust into the arena of spiritual warfare. What I want to do is to really take authority over any demonic force that would bring any harassment into your life so that we can have genuine assurance that you're going to be protected. Through prayer and intercession we want to provide a wall of protection around you.

J.W. I want to add something. The next day, after this happened, we were in my husband's pickup, and his clock, which is a computer clock, was off six hours from his watch. His watch said 1:33; the clock said 7:33. Okay, he took it to the company where he had bought the truck and got the clock reset because he didn't know how to do it, and now it will not stay set. It goes back six hours off.

D.L. Always six hours?

J.W. It's always six hours, exactly to the minute. Plus, he was in the Ace Hardware store the other day, and they were asking him all about this. He was telling about his truck. Talk about coincidences! There was a man that came up to him and said, "I overheard you talking about your truck, the clock in your truck. My dad's truck ... he lives up in that area. His clock was off six hours, and he had taken it and had it reset, and it goes back six hours again."

D.L. He's up in that same area where you saw the UFO?

J.W. Yes. So there are two clocks that I know of that are off six hours. It was strange for them to be in the store at the same time and tell the story.

D.L. Yes, another of those coincidences...

J.W. That was a strange thing.

D.L. There are too many coincidences.

J.W. Yeah, there are.

D.L. I don't know what to make of it, but...

J.W. Well, see that kind of — trying to weigh this all out myself, you know, trying to decide, is this being from another planet, or is this demonic? I felt like I was a judge caught in the middle, you know, deciding which. I put that down as evidence of the demonic side because of the number six. And if you add six hours either way . . . say it's one o'clock and you add six hours; it comes out to seven. If you subtract six hours, it comes out to seven. I don't care what time, it will be the same time. So there is a confusion of not knowing if the clock is ahead or behind. You do that on other numbers and it doesn't work. But that's strange. I took that as a clue to the six meaning Satan. You know, that's his number. Then also by my dream of that casket; to me that represented death.

And then there is one more thing I want to tell you, and I don't think this lady would mind. She called me. Her name is Mabel Sloan. And she called me one morning, and she said, "I saw the same thing you girls did." Whether she did or not I don't know. But it was the same morning, and she said she was awakened out of her sleep, and there was this bright light in her room; the walls were bright. And so she sat up in bed. And she said then an orange glow came by her window and it shined across on the other walls. You know, she said, about the pace of someone walking. And then another light followed it. And then the room became dark; it was gone. So she went to the front door and looked out, and she said there were no police cars or ambulances or anything like that. There was no sound at all and nothing out there. And she looked at her clock, and it said twelve after five, that same morning.

D.L. Talk about strange.

J.W. And then she went on to tell me, "Now, I don't know if this has any meaning or not. I am a Christian woman, and I don't go for any foolishness." You know, she was really at a loss for words. She remembered having had a dream about two months ago. In her dream she saw an object falling from the sky into her front yard. She went to her front door and looked out. She remembered thinking, in her dream, *That looks like an old snake skin, like when a snake sheds its skin.* Then she woke up. She said, "I don't know if that has any meaning or not."

To me it did. To me it represented Satan, the serpent falling out of heaven, and that snake skin was his covering. He lost his covering.

D.L. What does that mean? That Satan is going to be exposed?

J.W. He's either going to be exposed, or he's going to grow a new skin.

D.L. I have long believed that there will be alleged alien beings who will approach governmental leaders and offer solutions. This *glasnost — perestroika,* pulling down the wall, isn't going to last. What we have is an open window of opportunity in the Church to get the gospel out. If Jesus hasn't come back in the next few years, things are going to tighten up in the world. Problems are going to get worse. There could be an economic collapse. We're going to see and hear about alien beings coming to offer solutions to world leaders. Now this could be after the rapture or it could be before. They will offer solutions to the leadership of the world, and it's going to be accepted. I'm not saying this is the way the Antichrist comes to power, but it's one piece of the puzzle. It might be a bigger factor than we can envision right now. I am going to be cautious about making any predictions, but I will say that UFOs are a part of the end-time demonic delusion.

J.W. They're believing it's from some other planet.

D.L. It's *Star Trek* all the way, you know. This book [Referring to one of many books I had brought for Joanne to read] I've only mentioned to you because I wanted you to see that somebody outside of the religious realm was saying the same thing. If you have a need for this, you can borrow it. But protect it carefully as I don't know if it can be replaced.

D.L. Joanne, what's your educational background?

J.W. High school. Then I took a real estate course and add a lot of just practical business and life experience.

D.L. I can tell you're a bright person.

J.W. Well, thank you.

D.L. I want you to read this book first. The rest of them, read in any order you want to. You will notice books here by Dr. Clifford Wilson, by Zola Levitt, and John Weldon. They are all Christian writers. So is Kelly Seagraves. They all agree with my conclusions. Other authors are secular and present varying views.

When you're finished just give them to Mary.

If Jane were sitting here right now, would she have anything substantial to add? Or any other point of view?

J.W. Well, I don't think she'd have anything to add, and as far as, you know, thinking demonic, it's now beginning to soak in her head a little bit. At first she said, "Oh, it just couldn't be that." You see, to her it's alien beings from another planet.

D.L. Joanne, we are in the major age of deception. And the delusion is going to take so many forms as to be astounding.

J.W. But I haven't really convinced her it's possible, you know. [Referring to her friend and the demonic explanation of UFOs.]

D.L. Do you think it would be profitable for me to sit and talk to her as well at some future time?

J.W. Probably. I might just have her over when you come back.

[Note: I later talked to Jane Doe for almost three hours. I thought that she was agreeing with me. She has since rejected my point of view, according to a later interview she gave to the *Springfield News-Leader* daily newspaper. It is possible she just has not made up her mind on the subject. Perhaps she believes they are aliens from another world. If she has changed her mind recently, I am not aware of it — one way or the other.]

[End of interview.]

Mary Ramsey called on April 26, 1991 to alert me to media reports of cattle mutilations in Arkansas, around her area. The Ramseys own and operate a small factory just out of Harrison. The media reported the opinion of some who attribute the mutilations and organ removals to UFO activity. This is a concept widely reported along with accounts of animal mutilation cases in many places. Others said that Satanic cult activity should more likely be blamed for the mutilations. We are investigating these reports.

CHAPTER FIVE

UFO DELUSION

VS. THE GENESIS RECORD

ORIGIN OF MAN

A most sublime statement is found on the first page of the Bible: "In the beginning God created the heavens and the earth..." (Gen. 1:1). This statement establishes a worldview, a perception of reality, that affects every aspect of our lives. Man the creature is given to understand that he has obligations to God the Creator. The Bible reveals that man is to worship God and to have fellowship with Him. The apostle Paul wrote to the Roman Church:

> *Who is the blessed and only Potentate, the King of Kings, and Lord of Lords; Who only hath immortality, dwelling in the light which no man can approach unto; Whom no man hath seen, nor can see: To whom be honor and power everlasting. Amen (1 Tim. 6:15,16).*

The last book of the Bible describes a mighty angel who flies through the heavens crying with a loud voice, thus denoting the importance of his message:

> *And I saw another angel fly in the midst of heaven, having the everlasting gospel to preach unto them that dwell on the earth, and to every nation, and kindred, and tongue, and people, Saying with a loud voice, Fear God, and give glory to him; for the hour of*

his judgment is come: and worship him that made heaven, and earth, and the sea, and the fountains of waters (Rev. 14:6,7).

Worship the Creator! That is the angel's message. Anything Satan, the arch foe of God, can do to prevent this worship from taking place advances his deceptive and nefarious cause. Mankind is to worship the Creator who made all things!

Genesis 1:1 declares the existence of the personal, active, purposeful Creator. The universe did not just evolve, nor does it have an independent existence. It is not eternally going through cycles of death and rebirth. The universe and all that is in it began with the creative agency of the eternal God. He spoke the universe into existence by His own creative Word.

This biblical creation view, which has been embraced both by Judaism and Christianity, stands in direct contradiction against the assumptions of all other religions or philosophies. Other religious philosophies which hold that the universe itself is eternal negate the idea of a personal Creator. The New Age, Eastern mystics, and UFO advocates preach an impersonal life force. Man is his own god. There is no need for a redeemer, for there is no sin. One may use meditative or other techniques to descend into the lower depths of consciousness and there discover the divine within.

The idea that we are being visited by extraterrestrials from advanced planetary civilizations fits very well into most forms of Eastern Mysticism. God is no longer God but a force, a universal mind, a collective consciousness. The blind influence of karma (negative vibrations) with its hopeless cycles of reincarnation becomes the controlling principle behind the destiny of all things. The individual ceases to be important. Only the universal soul matters. If we do not accept Genesis, we cannot comprehend our origin, our potential nobility, nor our glorious destiny.

Earth is not evil; it is good: "The earth is the Lord's and the fulness thereof; the world, and they that dwell therein"

(Ps. 24:1; see 1 Cor. 10:26-28).

"Behold, the heaven and the heaven of heavens is the Lord's thy God, the earth also, with all that therein is" (Deut. 10:14).

Earth is good! The Bible demonstrates the character of the creation. Repeatedly in Chapter One of Genesis, the creation is called "good." When man was created in God's image, he was called "very good."

From this we know that God made His creation perfect. Man was morally undefiled. God not only made a good universe but has far-reaching and noble purposes for His creation.

The character of the Creator is shown in His creation. One has only to gaze at the heavens and the earth around him to discover God's awesome power and wisdom. No wonder strange ideas are being used to undermine these basic truths. It is true that the creation was horribly damaged by the fall. Nevertheless we still find the glory of God declared around us! The Psalmist beautifully expresses this truth:

The heavens declare the glory of God; the skies proclaim the work of his hands. Day after day they pour forth speech; night after night they display knowledge. There is no speech or language where their voice is not heard. Their voice goes out into all the earth, their words to the ends of the world. In the heavens he has pitched a tent for the sun, which is like a bridegroom coming forth from his pavilion, like a champion rejoicing to run his course. It rises at one end of the heavens and makes its circuit to the other; nothing is hidden from its heat (Ps. 19:1-6; NIV).

Genesis 1:1 accurately reveals the origin of the heavens and the earth. God is the One who measures the nations as dust on a scale's measuring pan (Isa. 40:15). God is the One who can measure the width of the heavens with His hand (Isa. 40:12). He placed the stars, the planets, the galaxies in their set places, naming each one (Isa. 40:26). Paul describes the creation as a revelation to mankind, "since what may be known about God is plain to them, because God has made it plain to them. For since the creation of the world God's invisible qualities — his eternal power and divine nature — have been clearly seen, being understood from what has been made, so that men are without excuse" (Rom. 1:19,20;NIV).

Genesis reveals the purpose of God for mankind. Man was to exercise dominion over the earthly creation, as God's representative. Man was capable of this vocation before the fall. Adam was not a brutish cave man. He was a highly intelligent and noble being. God told man to be fruitful and multiply, thus delegating a creative agency to him. God told man to care for the place in which he placed him. This garden, Gan Eden, was perfect, beautiful to look upon, and filled with good things to eat. (Hebrew: Gan Eden: Garden of Eden).

Man was not left without human companionship. Eve, his lovely wife, was his constant companion and comfort before the fall. She was a full partner in all the fulfilling works assigned to Adam. She became the partner with whom Adam would commune on a unique and deep physical and spiritual level.

Adam and Eve were given an important commandment. God prohibited them from eating of the tree of the Knowledge of Good and Evil. Through obedience they would make a volitional choice to obey God and continue in unbroken fellowship with Him. This volitional choice is the very heart of worship and service to God. Out of man's innocence must come the exercise of mature choice. His undefiled created state must become moral goodness. God wanted fellowship with man based upon willing choice.

Creation is neither haphazard nor purposeless. No existential groping for meaning is necessary within the framework of biblical creationism. The Creator has wonderful plans for His creation. He desired the life of Adam and Eve to be richly rewarding and meaningful. The hint of immortality is given in the unspoken promise of the

Tree of Life. But before man could enter into the fullness of God's purposes, he had to choose eternal life or forbidden knowledge. True fellowship and love is always based on free moral agency. If incapable of choosing evil, man would be incapable of experiencing the Divine fellowship. If I could force you to "love" me, it would not be love but slavery. Before you can love me, you have to know the power to reject me. If I can force you to love me, then you are not free. You are my slave or a mechanical toy.

THE TRAGEDY OF MAN — DECEIVED AND FALLEN IN SIN

Man failed the test, as revealed in the third chapter of Genesis. This is the reason for the present sad condition of humanity. Eve was deceived by the serpent; then she persuaded Adam to partake of her rebellious act. The fall had both temporal and eternal consequences for all of us. What we see in the war-torn world today is not a manifestation of God's will, but a manifestion of humanity's rejection of the will of the Almighty.

Man's sin destroyed his relationship with God. His soul was stained, his nature corrupted! Paul laments,

For although they knew God, they neither glorified him as God nor gave thanks to him, but their thinking became futile and their foolish hearts were darkened (Rom. 1:20;NIV).

As it is written: There is no one righteous, not even one; there is no one who understands, no one who seeks God. All have turned away, they have together become worthless; there is no one who does good, not even one. Their throats are open graves; their tongues practice deceit. The poison of vipers is on their lips. Their mouths are full of cursing and bitterness. Their feet are swift to shed blood; ruin and misery mark their ways, and the way of peace they do not know. There is no fear of God before their eyes (Rom. 3:10-18;NIV).

What catastrophe could have caused this terrible fall? How could Adam and Eve have produced descendants so full of evil and so far removed from Eden? The Genesis record reveals the existence of an entity that had evil designs upon man and opposed God's plan for him. The serpent is revealed in the Apocalypse as the devil or Satan (Rev. 12:9; 20:2). He came to Eden to deceive Adam and Eve, our father and mother, and then to overthrow God's purpose for mankind.

Satan's strategy was to weave a web of deception, to cause a paradigm shift in the very perception of reality. To gain his ends Satan had to fool man about his origin, about the true nature of God and about the possible relationship between God and man. One's view of reality will direct every aspect of his or her life.

The serpent decided to lead man to a new view of reality. The new reality must be appealing to human rationality. It must seem plausible. The result was deadly deception. Satan's tactics are the same today. Perhaps they are more sophisticated and take on an aura of scientific respectability, but at the root the tactic is the same. Satan's principal means of warfare is deception:

"Satan himself is transformed into an angel of light" (2 Cor. 11:14).

Antichrist, who is empowered by the dragon, Satan, will work lying "miracles" to deceive:

"Even him, whose coming is after the working of Satan with all power and signs and lying wonders ..." (2 Thess. 2:9).

The false prophet also works deceptive, Satanic "miracles":

And I beheld another beast coming up out of the earth; and he had two horns like a lamb, and he spake as a dragon. And he exerciseth all the power of the first beast before him, and causeth the earth and them which dwell therein to worship the first beast, whose deadly wound was healed. And he doeth great wonders, so that he maketh fire come down from heaven on the earth in the sight of men, And deceiveth them that dwell on the earth by the means of those miracles which he had power to do in the sight of the beast ... (Rev. 13:11-14).

Satan uses subterfuge to bring humans into bondage to cause their own destruction. The modern day UFO manifestation is a powerful arm of hell's fraud squad. It plays a major role in the hellish hoaxes of the end days.

The Eden event established a pattern for the rest of time. The devil's current tactics are not new. He recycles the same error repeatedly. Read your Bible to be ready to withstand the end-time delusion (see 2 Cor. 2:11). In the Genesis record we see Satan leading Eve to question the "real" meaning of what God had said: "Surely God could not have meant 'that.' Don't take His word so literally, Eve. Look for the deeper, hidden meanings of what God says. Did God really say, 'You must not eat from any tree in the garden'?" (Gen. 2:1). Here we see Satan working with all subtlety. He probes. He questions. There follows the blatant lie, the open challenge to God's character and intention.

Eve's response shows that her knowledge of God's commandment was not accurate. Had Adam failed to teach her or had Eve failed to learn? We do not know. In either case, her ignorance was so very costly! There is no bliss in ignorance, only miss. We miss out in the things that God has prepared for us! Many people find the subject of UFOs uncomfortable, bizarre. They would like to avoid the subject. They laugh nervously. But it is too late for ignorance. The form of deception coming is so incredible that it defies our imagination now.

Getting back to the Genesis 3 account of the fall of Adam and Eve, we find that after his opening foray and the subtle questioning of God's word, Satan blatantly contradicts the Word of God:

"You will not surely die..." (v. 4). He casts doubt first about content and purpose, then about the truth of God's Word. Small doubt blossoms into full-blown skepticism! Next the serpent smears the character of God.

"For God knows that when you eat of it your eyes will be opened, and you will be like God, knowing good and evil" (v. 5). God is presented as deceptive and selfish, things of which Satan himself is really guilty.

Eve's new doubts about God's Word and character set her up for deception and rebellion. Her newly sophisticated rationality allowed her to maneuver around the commandment of God, and she sinned! Let us not be unduly harsh with Eve alone. Adam came into rebellion by an act of his free choice. Eve would die according to God's immutable Word. Understandably Adam did not want to give up the relationship that he had with Eve. He decided that fellowship with Eve was more important than fellowship with God! So the Bible teaches that Eve was deceived and that Adam fell.

We learn from this that Satan hates the Word of God. He hates man, the new creation of God. He loathes the fact that God has a blessed plan for redeemed humanity. He knows that our perception of reality, if based upon the Word of God, will contradict his lie. The Word of God allows man to correctly interpret all phenomena about Him.

For Satan to succeed in the last days, he must work a deception so subtle and so powerful that it will overwhelm the human race both with its rationality and attraction.

An offer by visitors from an advanced civilization on another planet for assistance to a perishing human race confronted with war, crime, violence, pollution, global warming, genocide, and a host of other ills that man's rebellion have produced will seem irresistible. That the mainstream scientific community is taking the UFO question seriously, as evidenced by the heavily-funded, government-sponsored SETI program, demonstrates that we must look at the subject in a very serious light. Any person who is well-grounded in the Bible and who takes the Word of God literally will not be prone to fall for the end-time delusion. The apostle Paul contrasts those who accept the Bible with those who reject it:

They perish because they refused to love the truth and so be saved. For this reason God sends them a powerful delusion so that they will believe the lie and so that all will be condemned who have not believed the truth but have delighted in wickedness. But we ought always to thank God for you, brothers loved by the Lord, because from the beginning God chose you to be saved through the sanctifying work of the Spirit and through belief in the truth. He called you to this through our gospel, that you might share in the glory of our Lord Jesus Christ (2 Thess. 2:10-14;NIV).

Satan hates the Bible because it reveals him for what he really is, a fallen creature who lost it all because of unbelief and pride. The Bible record of his fall is abhorrent to him. Both Isaiah and Ezekiel contribute to our picture of that hour of heavenly rebellion and its consequences:

You were the model of perfection, full of wisdom and perfect in beauty. You were in Eden, the garden of God; every precious stone adorned you: ruby, topaz and emerald, chrysolite, onyx and jasper, sapphire, turquoise and beryl. Your settings and mountings were made of gold; on the day you were created they were prepared. You were anointed as a guardian cherub, for so I ordained you. You were on the holy mount of God; you walked among the fiery stones. You were blameless in your ways from the day you were created till wickedness was found in you. Through your widespread trade you were filled with violence, and you sinned. So I drove you in disgrace from the mount of God, and I expelled you, O guardian cherub, from among the fiery stones. Your heart became proud on account of your beauty, and you corrupted your wisdom because of your splendor (Ezek. 28:12-17;NIV).

How you have fallen from heaven, O morning star [Lucifer — KJV], *son of the dawn! You have been cast*

down to the earth, you who once laid low the nations!
You said in your heart, "I will ascend to heaven; I will
raise my throne above the stars of God; I will sit
enthroned on the mount of assembly, on the utmost
heights of the sacred mountain. I will ascend above
the tops of the clouds; I will make myself like the Most
High." But you are brought down to the grave, to the
depths of the pit (Isa. 14:12-15;NIV).

Satan also hates the Bible because it foretells his doom!

And the devil, who deceived them, was thrown into
the lake of burning sulfur, where the beast and the
false prophet had been thrown. They will be tormented
day and night for ever and ever (Rev. 20:10;NIV).

He hates the Bible because it reveals to man how he can
obtain salvation. To reach his goals, Satan cannot allow
mankind to experience the fulfillment of the promises of
God. He must thwart God's plans and prevent the promises
of God from coming to pass. The devil now knows that he
is doomed. In his rage he desires to drag the human race
down in ruin and damnation. He still wants to prove God
wrong, though he knows there is no hope for his future. Or
is it possible that the prince of devils still harbors an insane
hope of fomenting a further rebellion against the Almighty
this time with a hope of success?

If the latter proposition is true, then Satan could reason
that if God can be proved a liar because even one of His
promises fails to come to pass, then God cannot be just and
judge Satan for pride and rebellion. The only way Satan
can do this is to prevent man from going over to the other
side. He must blind man and bind him in total rebellion so
that all mankind will be destroyed and so that God cannot
finally fulfill His Word! Paul writes of the great rescue that
God has undertaken through Jesus Christ:

For he has rescued us from the dominion of darkness
and brought us into the kingdom of the Son he loves,

in whom we have redemption, the forgiveness of sins (Col. 1:13,14;NIV).

In writing to the church in Corinth, Paul also revealed that Satan is blinding people in darkness so that they will perish:

> *And even if our gospel is veiled, it is veiled to those who are perishing. The god of this age has blinded the minds of unbelievers, so that they cannot see the light of the gospel of the glory of Christ, who is the image of God* (2 Cor. 4:3,4;NIV).

John saw what would be the final step of Satan's efforts, in the end-times, to involve mankind in an ultimate rebellion to lead them to their destruction:

> *A third angel followed them and said in a loud voice: "If anyone worships the beast and his image and receives his mark on the forehead or on the hand, he, too, will drink of the wine of God's fury, which has been poured full strength into the cup of his wrath. He will be tormented with burning sulfur in the presence of the holy angels and of the Lamb. And the smoke of their torment rises for ever and ever. There is no rest day or night for those who worship the beast and his image, or for anyone who receives the mark of his name"* (Rev. 14:9-11;NIV).

Satan is eaten with jealousy when he thinks that man will forever enjoy what he rejected and lost. Imagine the puny creature, man, ruling with God, one day judging his infernal majesty himself! We will give voice in agreement with God's pronouncement of doom upon Satan. We will rule with the Lord from the throne and as co-regents with Jesus.

> *Do you not know that the saints will judge the world? And if you are to judge the world, are you not competent to judge trivial cases? Do you not know that we will judge angels? How much more the things of this life!* (1 Cor. 6:2,3;NIV).

*To him who overcomes, I will give the right to sit
with me on my throne, just as I overcame and sat
down with my Father on his throne* (Rev. 3:21;NIV).

*I saw thrones on which were seated those who had
been given authority to judge* (Rev. 20:4;NIV).

To pull off his hellish scheme, Satan must deceive
humanity. The biblical ideas of the origin of man, the
nature of God and the possible relationship of the two must
be toppled. As noted, Eve was deceived by Satan's challenge
of God's revealed Word. Through the theory of evolution
and by means of the new end-time UFO\E.T. delusion,
Satan hopes to deceive us. The Bible teaches that man was
created a noble creature made in the image of God. This
image is moral and spiritual. Man had the capacity for
fellowship, love, worship, and faith, all uniquely human
qualities of the spiritual nature of man pointing to the God
who created him.

There are leading scientists and politicians as well as
Eastern mystics who now teach that Earth is being visited
by beings vastly superior to us, far advanced in their
evolution. The aliens are here for benevolent purposes
(Some disagreement on that point exists). They come with
a message of salvation. Soon they will raise up a human
leader in our midst who will be endowed with special
abilities and wisdom. This man will lead the world into a
New Age of peace and prosperity. Wars will be abolished,
pollution conquered, hunger done away with, and the
universal fellowship of man will prevail.

EVOLUTION — FOUNDATION FOR DECEPTION

In 1859 a powerful deception concerning the nature of
man arose through Charles Darwin who popularized the
uniformitarian theory of evolution. His book, *The Origin of
the Species,* became an overnight best seller. All 1,250
copies of the book were sold out on the first day of publication,
much to the surprise of both Darwin and his publisher!

Later, George Bernard Shaw, an agnostic, made an

insightful comment concerning Darwin and his theory. He said that the world was waiting for Charles Darwin. He posited that humanity longed for a theory with a cloak of scientific credibility that would allow man to throw off the dominion of God. It was the "Invictus" for all non-Christian humans. Shaw's perception of the influence of Darwin and his eager followers was correct.

Extreme views of uniformitarian evolution provide a deceptive theory to explain the nature of man outside biblical revelation, and in the process they can deny the very Creator himself! As noted earlier, in 1952, while a college student, one of the authors of this book postulated the idea that at some future date there would be a deception comparable in strength to Darwin's theory of evolution. Darwin had thrust forth a new idea about the origin and nature of man. For the end-time deception to be complete, there would have to be a theory that would also deny the true nature of God. Thus would be completed the circle of deception. We will later examine the second phase of the deception and its relation to the UFO/E.T. hypothesis. Indeed we are looking at a masterstroke of satanic genius. *Star Wars,* the "force"; *E.T.; Close Encounters of the Third Kind;* "Alf"; *Star Trek;* "Star Man"; UFO "fact" documentaries; and a myriad of UFO books and publications have all made their contribution to the delusion.

"The lie" presents man as only another beast of the field, a little more advanced, but a beast nevertheless. This lie is called the theory of evolution, a pseudo scientific term. Perhaps the "religion of evolution" is a more appropriate designation.

A scientific theory must have observable evidence that can be correlated into a cohesive and reasonable speculation as to their united underlying principle or law. Evolution lacks such a united body of evidence! How can observable data be gathered about an event, the beginning of the universe, that is so far in the past as to be unobservable? Even so, man has accepted and taught evolution as truth.

Once evolution replaced creation in mankind's world-view, man no longer felt himself to be under obligation to God. He was, after all, only a cell that has mutated into a higher life form. But evolution leaves some great questions unanswered: Does life have meaning? What is the purpose of existence? Since the Bible is rejected, answers must be sought and found elsewhere.

When man denies his status as a creation of a loving God, he does become a beast in his thought and actions. All the evil that man does is from his bondage to the flesh nature that causes him to act as a beast would act. Evolution also denies sin's consequences. There is no logical place for a personal God in such a system of belief. Therefore, there is no such thing as sin. If there is no sin, then what need do we have of Jesus? It follows that the gospel is only another one of humanity's inventions, an especially bad one because it hinders one from reaching full potential. Biblical Christianity, once highly revered, becomes the ultimate enemy and must be altered or eliminated.

If ye be reproached for the name of Christ, happy [are ye]; for the spirit of glory and of God resteth upon you: on their part he is evil spoken of, but on your part he is glorified (1 Pet. 4:14).

And many shall follow their pernicious ways; by reason of whom the way of truth shall be evil spoken of (2 Pet. 2:2).

The so-called "theory" of evolution is part of a world-view that Satan presents as an alternative to the biblical world-view. If the nature of man is denied, if man does not need to concern himself with the problem of sin, then the nature of God can also be denied. God the Creator is rejected and put out of the frame of reference held dear by modern secular man. This is the first step toward the end-time delusion.

Satan must present a soothing explanation for the

concept of God. God is presented as impersonal, a force that drives man on toward an evolutionary goal. This idea was inherent in Satan's lie to Eve: "...and you will be like God..." Man is elevated and God is demoted. God is no longer thought to be greater than the material universe. He is simply an impersonal part of it. He is the "force" (as in the *Star Wars* movie trilogy) that has its dark side and its light side. It is the stream of impersonal energy that anyone can tap into for good or for ill. Man then thinks himself capable of growing into a divine state. In fact, man is believed to be a part of the deity-force.

The future Satan offers man is an evolutionary future. It results in continuous cycles of reincarnation. According to this Eastern world-view, which has now all but overwhelmed Western Christian civilization, all of us will keep coming back ("You will not surely die...") until we enter into the blank all nothingness of nirvana or enter a highly-evolved Godlike state. Before our wondering eyes blooms a new aspect of Satan's lie. There are beings who have already achieved this Godlike level of evolution, and they are in contact with us!

THE UFO CONNECTION

The very idea of beings from other worlds is fascinating. If the Bible is not the source of truth, then something must be offered to explain miracles, mystical occurrences, alleged extraterrestrial contacts (close encounters of the third kind) and the mystery of man's origin and destiny. The evolutionary UFO religion provides this: all miracles are supposedly the result of the activities of superior beings from other worlds. Early man in his ignorance ascribed deity to these visitors from other planets; thus, an explanation of angels, demons, devils, and even God himself emerges. The Bible is thought to be a result of early man's misunderstanding of alien visitations. Unable to comprehend the scope and nature of the universe, incapable of conceiving of other humanoids from far distant worlds, man reacted to these alien visitors by writing down myths, legends, and fanciful tales, all of which got compiled in the Bible and other "sacred" writings. This is a view commonly held in the secular world today.

Unexplained events are also said to be the result of "aliens" in contact with the world. In this alternative religion, man is evolving as did these aliens. Since they have been evolving for eons of time longer than man, they are advanced far beyond us. They have been observing us for a long time. Now, they have decided we are ready for the next step of advancement. They are here to help us to attain the next evolutionary leap into a spiritual transformation that will usher in a new age! So the truth of God is replaced with the lie, a lie so enormous that Bible-believing Christians find it hard to believe that it exists, but a lie that is well-publicized and has potent appeal to a materialistic world.

DESTINY OF REDEEMED MANKIND

Opposed to this view of man's future, the Bible presents a future that, compared to endless cycles of karma, is glorious and wonderful to consider. God is not an impersonal force that energizes the materialistic creation. He is a personal, loving Creator and Redeemer with whom redeemed humanity is destined to dwell forever!

Then I saw a new heaven and a new earth, for the first heaven and the first earth had passed away, and there was no longer any sea. I saw the Holy City, the new Jerusalem, coming down out of heaven from God, prepared as a bride beautifully dressed for her husband. And I heard a loud voice from the throne saying, "Now the dwelling of God is with men, and he will live with them. They will be his people, and God himself will be with them and be their God. He will wipe every tear from their eyes. There will be no more death or mourning or crying or pain, for the old order of things has passed away." He who was seated on the throne said, "I am making everything new!" Then he said, "Write this down, for these words are trustworthy and true" (Rev. 21:1-5;NIV).

This is no evolutionary pipe dream! It is a glorious reality, an eternal future with the personal, loving Creator!

I did not see a temple in the city, because the Lord God Almighty and the Lamb are its temple. The city does not need the sun or the moon to shine on it, for the glory of God gives it light, and the Lamb is its lamp. The nations will walk by its light, and the kings of the earth will bring their splendor into it. On no day will its gates ever be shut, for there will be no night there. The glory and honor of the nations will be brought into it. Nothing impure will ever enter it, nor will anyone who does what is shameful or deceitful, but only those whose names are written in the Lamb's book of life. Then the angel showed me the river of the water of life, as clear as crystal, flowing from the throne of God and of the Lamb down the middle of the great street of the city. On each side of the river stood the tree of life, bearing twelve crops of fruit, yielding its fruit every month. And the leaves of the tree are for the healing of the nations. No longer will there be any curse. The throne of God and of the Lamb will be in the city, and his servants will serve him. They will see his face, and his name will be on their foreheads. There will be no more night. They will not need the light of a lamp or the light of the sun, for the Lord God will give them light. And they will reign for ever and ever. The angel said to me, "These words are trustworthy and true. The Lord, the God of the spirits of the prophets, sent his angel to show his servants the things that must soon take place." "Behold, I am coming soon! Blessed is he who keeps the words of the prophecy in this book" (Rev. 21:22-22:7;NIV).

Will you respond to this offer of eternal life today?

The Spirit and the bride say, "Come!" And let him

who hears say, "Come!" Whoever is thirsty, let him come; and whoever wishes, let him take the free gift of the water of life (Rev. 22:17;NIV).

If you would like to experience new life in Jesus Christ as the Saviour of your soul, you can begin to know Him right now by calling upon Him. Simply reach out to Him in faith and ask Him to forgive you, to save you and to live in your heart!

CHAPTER SIX

CHARIOTS OF THE FRAUDS

In the late 1950s Russian scientists offered a theory to explain events in the Bible, such as the destruction of Sodom and Gomorrah. They claimed that, while the account was basically true, the idea that Jehovah God had destroyed the cities because of their sins should no longer be accepted. These scientists proposed that it was aliens that rescued Lot and that after his deliverance, their spaceship had an atomic accident, exploding and destroying the valley of Sodom. Von Daniken, author of *The Chariots of the Gods,* accepts this idea and repeats it in his books. Some years later a boastful Russian cosmonaut would mockingly say that he had looked for God during his trip outside our planet's atmosphere but had not found Him — as if from his limited view he could observe the entire universe and so rule out the possibility of God's existence!

Our own astronauts have reported seeing UFOs, and some of them even believe in New Age-UFO ideas. The movie, *The Right Stuff,* portrayed John Glenn's encounter with little, firefly-like lights that danced around his capsule as aborigines danced and chanted below him in Australia. The implied idea in this scene is that shamanism and UFOs are connected! Another sighting was reported during the space voyage of Gemini 7. The television program "In Search of Ancient Mysteries" quoted NASA's Gemini 7

astronauts saying, "We have a bogey at 10 o'clock high..."
(A bogey is an unidentified craft. This sighting was made
in outer space so one assumption that has been made is
that it was a UFO.) These are only a few of the instances
when astronauts have either seen or expressed their belief
in the UFO phenomenon.

Mankind's entry into space with all the potential new
discoveries and new frontiers to explore has prompted
people to begin wondering seriously if there may not be
many other worlds with intelligent life upon them. Some
have even advanced the idea that our world has been
visited by ancient astronauts from other worlds. What is
the common point that connects these diverse events into
a world-view? Is there a relationship between Russian
speculation concerning Sodom and Gomorrah and *The
Right Stuff*? The connection of these modern events and
the ancient astronaut theory, which von Daniken
popularized and now many others have accepted, is found
in the evolutionary world-view.

Von Daniken claims that ancient astronauts have visited
and even colonized planet Earth. His theory proposes that
our development as a race is the direct result of alien
genetic manipulation and experimentation. He has become
one of the most popular proponents of this UFO theory.
Darwin's theory denied man's true origin and nature. Man
became an evolutionary product of blind chance. In recent
years, since the 1950s, the evolutionary theory of Darwin
has developed into the next stage in the shift of man's
world-view away from biblical creationism. The UFO
theories deny God's nature. God is no longer Deity, but
simply a being from an advanced technological, outer-
space civilization.

Why is mankind so intrigued and driven to seek answers
for his origin, apart from God's existence? The reason is
that man does not want to be under obligation as a creature
to his Creator! Mankind was ready for Darwin in the
1800s. Men were looking for a way to throw off the status
of a being created in God's image. In our day mankind is

ready for the UFO theory. Man wants to throw off the very idea of God and worship himself as God. Von Daniken's book, *The Chariots of the Gods*, and subsequent books have sold millions of copies. He has struck a responsive chord, much as Darwin did one hundred years earlier. A very long process of evolution is the underlying assumption behind the ancient astronauts' theory. There must have been an extremely long period from the beginning of the universe to the present. There are reasons for this. The first is that they must have had time to evolve beyond our own level of civilization. The second is the immense time required to travel the distances involved between Earth and most of the galaxies in the universe. According to one theory, they came from another galaxy to colonize our planet when their solar system died. The distances for such travel are themselves prohibitive. Intergalactic travel from such distances even at the speed of light makes this a nearly impossible speculation. The third is that pre-UFO-contact man on Earth must have evolved to a point at which aliens could do something meaningful to promote his development into modern man. But scientific evidence suggests a young creation, not an old one as demanded by Darwin's and von Daniken's theories. (For a more detailed study of this, please read Appendix 1.)

As time has gone on without satisfactory theories being proposed, more people are searching for some outside agency in the evolutionary process.

More and more scientists today are raising questions about the standard Darwinian theory of evolution, with its many gaps and contradictions. The new cult of space writing contends that the older theories of evolution can no longer be taken seriously, and so another type of evolutionary theory must be found to replace the one that has failed. These writers move evolution outward in space and backward in time, maintaining that human evolution took place in other worlds and its products were transported to the earth in extraterrestrial space vehicles. The only evidence for this strange notion is the supposed evidence that men of high technological skills lived on Earth in ancient times.[1]

Von Daniken has sought to deal with the failure of science to find an acceptable naturalistic explanation for life. He has proposed a theory of evolution that does not depend on chance, but upon the agency of outside intelligences — ancient astronauts who visited and colonized our planet. Keep in mind that his theory of the origin of modern man does not answer the question of ultimate origins: From where did these alien visitors come and when and where did life begin? If there must have been a beginning and a Prime Originator, why not accept the biblical view? Which makes more sense considering all the evidence? Concerning the UFO theory, Jacques Vallee observes,

A fascinating aspect of the study of these phenomena is that no theory of their origin and nature can be constructed without reference to theories of the origin of man and the nature of life.[2]

These theories that there were ancient astronauts are not scientific. A theory that deals with the origins and meaning of life is really a religion. Darwinian evolution itself has little data to recommend it as a scientific theory. It is more properly a religion dressed in a lab coat. The UFO religion also dresses in pseudo-scientific garb in an attempt to avoid the religion label. But religion it is nevertheless. Evidently, von Daniken himself believes this to be true.

Despite all accusations, von Daniken is regarded by multitudes as a sort of "new messiah." Recent studies point thousands as ready to accept von Daniken's theories as a new religion. The author was even quoted as saying that a new religion will emerge, a religion explaining God in patterns suggested in his writings.[3]

Some who accept his theories have become New Age

"evangelists" for this new religion that von Daniken has promoted.

His religion is one that he hopes will overthrow and replace biblically-revealed truth. He has a definite hatred of the Bible and scorns those who believe it. Von Daniken believes that the Bible is stupid, as are those who believe it. Speaking of American believers he says,

Here they are so crazy about Christ, and they don't know the truth, and they don't want to know the truth, you know. They believe the Bible is the word of God. This is after studying the story, so stupid that I can't understand how somebody can believe it.[4]

He hopes that his "truth" will replace the Bible so that mankind is "free" to receive new information. In effect, if men hate the truth of the Bible, they will be open to believe a lie! He says,

I am not sure, but my idea is that now we lose religion, more or less, with our research more and more people lose religion, they just find out that what they had been told is not true, so the brain is free now for other information or reception...[5]

Von Daniken has rejected the Bible and has opened himself to the occult practices of this UFO religion. How did he become convinced of its veracity? He obtained this revelation during an astral projection, a recognized occult practice! New Age author Brad Steiger writes,

Erich von Daniken himself has stated that the theory came to him on an astral trip, and that he knows himself to be a reincarnated ancient astronaut.[6]

A researcher of Easter Island archaeology, Edmundo Edwards, was told by von Daniken, "The public wants to read books about people from outer space — so that's what I write about." In the preface to the book, *Some Trust in Chariots,* the editors write,

For now that the human race is treading the brink

*of total disaster by ecological upset or by nuclear war,
a book that can point to the probability of
extraterrestrial aid in the past may also imply the
hope of extraterrestrial aid in the terrifying future. If,
that is to say, the reviewers whose praises ornament
the cover of the popular edition of the book are right.
If, however, they are wrong, then the book is at best
folly, and at worst a cruel delusion.*[7]

There is certainly a cruel hoax involved when men turn
from revealed, verifiable truth to myths with no evidence.
The worst thing about such New Age-UFO ideas, which
have proliferated since von Daniken's book first appeared,
is that they are based on a false foundation and yet are
believed by people with an evangelistic fervor.

CHARIOTS OF THE GODS?

Von Daniken's book, *The Chariots of the Gods*, proposes
the theory that ancient astronauts from another star
system landed on Earth a few millennia ago. Before they
came to this planet, according to the theory, civilization
was in a primitive stone age period with only basic stone
tools and no advanced technology. After their contact with
primitive humans and with the aid of genetic
experimentation, man's evolution took a giant leap forward.

To prove his theory, von Daniken tries to use the many
unsolved mysteries of our planet's and mankind's history.
But his book is so full of errors that one archaeologist
observed,

*Archaeologists, historians, linguists and scientists,
almost without exception, label von Daniken's book as
nonsense and say that it is consistently in error, both
as to the facts dealt with and their interpretation. Dr.
Herbert Alexander, professor of Archaeology at Simon
Fraser University in Burnaby, British Columbia,
commented that almost nothing in von Daniken's
book, related to archaeology, is factually correct.*[8]

One must ask — if von Daniken is so inaccurate, why

follow any of his theory? After all, we already have an explanation for mankind's origins and mankind's future in a book that has been shown to be accurate historically, scientifically, and most importantly, spiritually — we speak of the Bible!

Referring to the biblical account of the creation of man, von Daniken tells us that according to his "speculations" we can explain the sudden development of modern man only by postulating "unknown intelligences" that came to our world and artificially made major changes in our genetic code (Gods From Outer Space, p.26). It seems simpler to stick to biblical terminology and say that this was God's creative intervention.[9]

It is easy to take many divergent, unknown or unexplained mysteries of early Earth history and through conjecture and assumptions weave them into some kind of proof for a theory. But merely conjecturing or saying something is a fact does not make it a fact! Concerning this circuitous logic used by von Daniken,

In general one notices throughout his book a tendency to slip from establishing that a thing is possible to an assumption that it really exists and so can be used as a "proof" of his hypothesis (cf.p.20; p.106; p.167). He often encourages the reader to make the jump for himself by a loaded rhetorical question. At the same time, he attempts to forestall would-be critics of his theories by calling into question their competence, their openness to new ideas, their objectivity (cf.p.11; p.107; p.124).[10]

The insulting thing about his theory is that it assumes that ancient man was incapable of great accomplishments without outside help. True archaeological science has proven just the opposite. Ancient man had vast amounts of knowledge about our world. Some ancient technologies may have surpassed our own. They were excellent astronomers. Medical practices in some cultures included brain surgery. They were capable in architecture, mathematics, agronomy, and animal husbandry. Creative and documentary writing has been shown to have been used very early in history. There is very good evidence to show that a worldwide trade economy existed at the time of the Phoenicians and perhaps even before. This included the New World. (See the book *America, BC,* by Harvard professor Dr. Barry Fell.) We have to readjust our thinking about ancient man's level of economic and scientific development.

We simply have not discovered all the records of ancient history yet. It is presumptuous of us to think of the first millennia of man's existence as something less important simply because we are so ignorant of it. In fact, we do have a record of "pre-history" — in the Bible! The Bible sheds more light on ancient man, both ante- and post-diluvian, than any other document. The Bible reveals that the development of these early people was often equal to our own.

> *The early post-deluge peoples were not savages. They retained much of the ante-diluvial world's science and skill, as suggested by the remarkable scientific accuracy of the Bible. This knowledge was slowly lost down through the years until regained during the last 300 to 400 years.*[11]

Another author writes,

> *We must forget this idea that ancient people were primitive — with no ability. They had plenty of ability. They could build their great amphitheaters, such as the magnificent structure at Caesarea on the Mediterranean coast. They could build this great fortress on Masada, 1,500 feet up the mountain at the southern end of the Dead Sea. We are not surprised to find buildings and so much more high up on that mountain, because men were intelligent, and had technological skills and ingenuity from way back.*[12]

And still another author writes,

Obviously, however, if the first Genesis Men, created in the image of God, lived nine centuries, their fantastic achievements in astronomy, metallurgy, pyramid-building, and other areas would be understandable.[13]

Ancient cities had vast libraries, water and sewer systems, hot water heating systems, and other conveniences. Some of their ideas about passive heating and cooling of homes are only now being looked into for use in our newest building techniques. In the last forty-five years, ninety percent of our present technology has been discovered. Perhaps we are only now rediscovering things that ancient man took for granted!

The fact that early pre-flood man and the first generations of post-flood man lived so long enabled them to develop and pass on many discoveries. Biblical chronology demonstrates this ability to pass on first-hand knowledge from Adam up through Abraham's time when writing was in existence so that the knowledge of the ante-diluvians could be recorded. The lifespan of Adam overlapped Methuselah's, whose overlapped that of Noah. Noah's lifespan overlapped Shem's, and Shem's lifespan, that of Abraham.

Unfortunately many records of early man were not recorded on survivable media. Parchment and papyri decay eventually. Our own books will decay in two hundred years unless written on acid-free paper. Would some future civilization be able to find much of our history, except perhaps fast-food, foam-plastic containers? What would they think of us? Those ancient records that we are presently in possession of have not all been translated, and many others have yet to be discovered. We are confident that as new discoveries come to light, they will confirm the biblical record, as have past discoveries. Ancient man was not only skilled; he left enough evidence to show his high degree of development in the earliest years of Earth's history.

In spite of all evidence to the contrary, von Daniken assumes men did not have metal tools, written languages, or any other technologies until they were visited by highly evolved beings from space. He believes that early man was not even genetically the same as modern man before these visitors supposedly came and did genetic experiments. As we have noted in the appendix, evolutionary theories, either Darwinian or the UFO kind, both have serious problems because of the increasing evidence of a young universe. But we must deal with von Daniken's ideas because so much of his theory has become a foundation for later New Age theories about UFOs. People have been convinced of the veracity of New Age ideas in part because they accept the illogical ideas with which von Daniken has hoodwinked many.

Von Daniken's "evidence" is full of errors. We will look at a few major pieces of his evidence to show the errors that are at the very foundation of his theory.

THE GREAT PYRAMID

Pyramidology is a fascinating field of study. Various people through much of modern history have spent time trying to find a reason for the existence of such gigantic structures. Some pyramid theories concern themselves with supposed prophecies revealed in the length of the great hall and the placement of the different chambers of the Pyramid of Cheops. The supposed exact placement of these features and the measurements of the construction of this pyramid are less than precise, according to modern standards. Even so the Great Pyramid is an astounding artifact of the ancient Egyptian culture.

. Most of the speculative theories about the purpose of this structure have long ago been dismissed by archaeological research. The Great Pyramid was and is a burial chamber, as were the other pyramids. Von Daniken uses this structure to invent a scenario concerning ancient Egypt that will fit his ancient astronaut theory.

Von Daniken finds it inconceivable that ancient man could have built the Pyramid in less than 600 years unless he had help. He claims that the stones were an average weight of 12-20 tons. Because of this great weight, the ancients could not have moved them without the help of some super intelligent advanced society — spacemen. But the stones do not average 12-20 tons. In fact the average is 2.5 tons each. A man who has studied both the ancient Egyptian language and archaeology, Christopher Baker D.D., L.S.S., writes,

> *Some 2,300,000 stones, averaging about 2 1/2 tons each, went into the pyramid.*[14]

Could ancient man have moved them? These stones were easily managed by the technologies of the time. Ancient evidence exists to show Egyptians moved much larger objects. One stone pictograph shows the colossus of Djehutihotep being drawn on a sledge:

> *There is a vivid picture of a colossal statue, estimated to weigh about 60 tons, being hauled on a wooden sledge by 172 men.*[15]

This statue is twenty-four times heavier than the pyramid stones. If it were feasible to move it, as the pictograph illustrates, then the stones of the Pyramid were movable by a similar means. An engineer, Clive Houlsby writes,

> *Now 2 1/2-ton blocks are not so very difficult to move given determination and grit...For the probable conditions, the coefficient of static friction would range from .30 to .65 requiring about 20 men to manipulate each block, under average conditions.*[16]

Ancient records and modern science all point to the Egyptians building the Great Pyramid using their technologies, without spacemen to help them.

> *Every authority that has investigated the subject, including the ancient historian Herodotus, lacked hesitation in concluding that an intelligent people such as the ancient Egyptians, working with their primitive tools, would have difficulty in building it*

within about 20 years. Modern experts believe that only a few thousand seasonal laborers were employed. By taking advantage of the annual flooding of the Nile to ship the blocks of stone on barges and by levers, sledges, rollers and ramps, the work was simple. The Egyptians even left drawings in stone showing some methods used by them, but von Daniken did not think it necessary to mention this fact.[17]

Another area of speculation about the Great Pyramid in which von Daniken dabbles concerns mathematical formulas that he believes are hidden in the measurements of the structure itself. His claim is that these point to an advanced civilization, a civilization that was able to navigate the stars! This is so obviously erroneous that simple grade school mathematics can disprove it. Dr. Clifford Wilson quotes von Daniken:

"Is it really a coincidence that the height of the Pyramid of Cheops multiplied by 1,000 million corresponds approximately to the distance between the earth and sun? That is to say, 93 million miles."
[End of von Daniken quote by Wilson.]

[Wilson continues] *The calculation is easily made. The height of the Pyramid is 481.4 feet and there are 5,280 feet to a mile. Therefore the distance would be 91.17 million miles. If we are to accept von Daniken's statements about the fantastic accuracy of these ancient records we would expect a much closer degree of accuracy than that.*[18]

Our own space program has demonstrated the need for accuracy in measurements much closer than this for travel in the relatively short distances within our own solar system. The possibility of these interstellar travelers ever finding our planet would have been miraculous with such inaccuracy! It would be like trying to throw a dart at one particular grain of sand on a beach from an airplane, blindfolded!

In addition, why the number "1,000 million" (the British term for "one billion")? One billion is not a scientific standard of measurement or mathematical constant. There is no reason to choose it except it seems to give a number close to the astronomical unit, ninety-three million miles, the mean distance between the sun and Earth. The number 1,020.0254 million would provide a product equal to one A.U., but it would be so obvious a manipulation that he settles for the number one billion hoping no one will think to check out his mathematics![19]

Von Daniken claims that ancient astronauts were the source of the knowledge that went into the design and the building of the Great Pyramid. In another attempt to prove this, von Daniken claims that the mathematical constant *pi* is found in the measurement of the base area divided by twice the height. (This is 756 x 756= 571,536 then divided by 962, giving the figure of 594.1, not *pi* which is 3.1416.) Even using ancient measuring standards *pi* is not obtained through this calculation. There is no need to continue to demonstrate the errors in his knowledge concerning both mathematics and the antiquities of Egypt.

THE NAZCA PLAIN MARKINGS

There is an amazing area in Peru called the Nazca Plain. Upon this vast desert plateau are inscribed, an inch or two deep in the surface soil, great figures and geometric designs. This area is so arid that markings in the surface of the soil will probably remain indefinitely. Von Daniken claims that this area is a vast landing area for spaceships (according to his book) and a great map (according to a television special based upon his book) from which the space travelers obtained their bearings. The first thing that strikes us as curious about his claim is, that given the ground-imaging computer technologies that our own modern fighter aircraft use, why are these "maps" even necessary? Immovable landmarks, such as mountains or rivers, are used to direct an aircraft and cruise missiles or pinpoint satellite reconnaissance photos to within feet or inches! Could beings who can navigate the stars have any need of primitive drawings to navigate to a particular place on the Earth?

Second, the Nazca Plain is not the sort of place that aircraft could land upon very easily. The soil is dry and loose. The markings go up and down gullies — not a likely landing place for intelligent beings! Any aircraft taking off would have washed out the markings with jet blast or prop-wash. So these could not be runways. Third, the UFO "spacecraft" sighted by other people usually hover and lift off and land vertically. Why would they need runways? What are the markings if they are not a spacecraft landing area or a giant navigational landmark? One author observes,

> *Archaeologists also emphasize that the gigantic lines on the Nazca Plain in Peru were built for calendaric and astronomical purposes, not as landing strips. The markings go up and down steep ravines and no aircraft could land on them (not even aircraft making the television film based on von Daniken's book).* [20]

Another contention of von Daniken is that the markings could not be made without aerial observation. At first this seems to make sense. If he is right, this could explain other such monuments scattered around the world. There are other earth-mounds, earth-carvings, or earth-drawings that are built upon a gigantic scale like those of Nazca. How could the natives of Nazca have built them?

An example of a modern practice that shows this to be possible can be found in the grain fields of Kansas and Nebraska. There have been farmers who have planted huge fields with different varieties of plants to create a living painting. Once the plants germinate, their different colors and growth rates create a changing living picture throughout the growing season. One such painting was of a vase with flowers in it, a still life! How are they able to lay out and make these complicated designs? Do they have a friend hovering overhead in a helicopter radioing back instructions? Are they using satellites in outer space to give them an updated view from space? No, the method they use is very simple and totally effective. They do it by graphing out their acreage on a scaled-down plan. Then they execute it by laying out the plan on the fields using marking posts. If we can conceive of this without any trouble, why could those people in Nazca — and every other such place in the world where such markings have been made — not also have conceived of it?

ANCIENT TROY WAS NOT A MYTH

In the television program, "In Search of Ancient Mysteries," based largely on von Daniken's theory, there was an attempt to portray von Daniken in the same light as Heinrich Schliemann, who accepted Homer's Odyssey as a poetic, yet accurate account of an ancient city called Troy. (Von Daniken also mentions Schliemann in his book.) Schliemann found Troy based upon evidence found in Homer's work though he was mocked and thought foolish for believing that Troy was a real place. Is von Daniken another man who is rejected because he has such innovative ideas? Von Daniken is no Schliemann. He has not based his theory of the Nazca plain drawings, the Great Pyramid, or any other antiquity upon solid evidence, written records, or careful research. In fact he has ignored or twisted ancient written records because they do not agree with his theory.

What correlation is there between Troy and other ancient legends that have eventually proved to be fact and the theory of ancient astronauts? Absolutely none! It is not logical to suppose that just because the legend of Troy was proved to be true that von Daniken's idea is also true. Suppose we were to take a mathematics test. Would the whole class receive the grade of the highest student in the class simply because he was right? No, we would all have to pass the test individually. Yet this is precisely what von Daniken wants us to believe: that because Schliemann was right, he is also right.

Von Daniken is rejected not because he is another persecuted visionary, but because he is totally inaccurate in his facts and conclusions. He has flunked the test! Schliemann found Troy. Where is the discovery of an ancient UFO by von Daniken? There has been no demonstrable evidence of ancient astronauts! It is assumed they existed; then evidence is forced to fit the hypothesis. Troy existed and was located because a man found evidence and uncovered proof. He did not invent Troy and then go out to prove that an ancient city was Troy when in fact it was not Troy. Von Daniken has invented a theory and used every conceivable twist of logic to prove it. It is more properly science fiction than science!

He has not only attempted to force-fit the antiquities of ancient cultures of the past into his theory. He has also attempted to force accounts from the Bible into his theory. Remember, he believes the Bible is a stupid book. Why would he even worry about a "stupid" book? Perhaps he realizes that it is the one true challenge to his world-view that would demand that he turn from his error to the God of creation!

ARK OF THE COVENANT — A RADIO RECEIVER?

Von Daniken is not well-informed in biblical history and theology. He enters an area that he has not researched carefully. He attempts to twist the clearest statements of the Word of God to fit his theory. Like every other cultic speculator, he cannot ignore the Bible. Every cult is forced to deal with this amazing Book because it is the one opposing voice to the vain philosophies of the world. His only choice, then, is to try to present the Bible in a way that will fit his theory. One writer concerned about the ancient spaceman hoax observes,

In this wild orgy of speculation, the biblical ark of the covenant is posed as an electrically charged condenser and loudspeaker, the Noahic Flood and the

destruction of Sodom and Gomorrah as the deliberate
extermination of unsuccessful breeding experiments,
and Ezekiel's "living creatures" and "wheels within
wheels" as space ships.[21]

Von Daniken claims the ark was a radio receiver and that it also stored a charge of electricity sufficient to kill a person who touched it. One of the authors of this book (R.L.S.) was trained in electronics and has had years of experience in electronics repair both in the U.S. navy and civilian life. The contention that the ark and the cherubim were a radio device is absolutely silly. For a circuit to be able to receive transmitted signals, much more than a condenser and a speaker are necessary. There would also have to be an antenna of some sort to receive the signal. A circuit designed to change the FM, AM, short-wave, or any other transmission signal into audio frequency waves would be necessary. And there would have to be an output circuit that would amplify the audio signal sufficiently to drive a speaker coil and generate a sound wave in the air.

It is unbelievable that an advanced alien society would use a primitive receiver such as von Daniken describes in the first place. Consider the microchip transmitters and receivers we have today. Some of them can fit inside a raisin. Beings, if they existed, that could travel at the speed of light would undoubtedly have better technology than he describes. Would a large, heavy box make sense if aliens wanted to communicate with mankind?

Besides this, the ark could never have worked as a condenser. A condenser is an electrical-charge storage device; another name for a condenser is a capacitor. There must be two plates separated by a non-conducting dielectric material. The size of the plates and the effectiveness of the dielectric material determine the capacity of the condenser. The ark was overlaid completely inside and out with pure gold. Gold is one of the best conductors in existence. This means that there would not be an ability for the ark to act as a condenser because every square inch of the ark would be electrically conductive with every other square inch.

Neither could the "mercy seat" serve as a separate plate because it was solid gold, resting in physical and electrical contact with the gold of the ark. The whole would short circuit continually so as to never build up a charge. If the earth and the ark were the two plates separated by air, then anyone who would touch the ark, including priests, would have been electrocuted. Also, every time the ark was set down, it would discharge with the ground.

Finally, it isn't only the voltage that kills; it is the voltage and the amperage. A static charge of several thousand volts can build up on a person when winter weather dries out the air. Have you touched a door knob in the dark only to see a blue spark jump? That is a charge of several thousand volts. It is non-lethal because of the low amperage. (Do not touch a computer with such a charge because you may wipe out a chip. They are much more sensitive to low amperage charges than people.) A charge of static electricity sufficient to kill would have to be enormous, such as the millions of volts in lightning. This would require very effective insulation between the ark and the ground and between the ark and the people who would carry it to allow for the ark to be handled.

Air can also serve as an insulator at the rate of thousands of volts per inch, depending upon humidity. If air was the only insulation, the ark would have had to float dozens of feet in the air to be kept from discharging through the nearest person or into the earth! Of course this is preposterous. Neither did von Daniken know anything about the content of Bible passages concerning the ark.

Von Daniken says on page 40 of his book, "Without actually consulting Exodus, I seem to remember..." This is an astounding admission ...[22]

Indeed it is astounding that anyone who wanted to propose a theory about the origin of man, the ark of the covenant, the ancient civilizations of the Earth would do so without seriously studying the source materials — in the case of man's origin and the ark.

EZEKIEL'S VISION OF GOD

Von Daniken claims that the vision Ezekiel saw by the River Kebar in Babylon was a spacecraft and that God is a spaceman. According to him it is preposterous that God would travel by such a conveyance as described by Ezekiel in the first chapter of his prophecy. (It would be good to refresh your memory by reading Chapter One of Ezekiel.) The words used by Ezekiel give us a clear indication that he was not looking at a physical phenomenon, but at a vision.

A vision will convey a literal truth, but the Lord's presence is such that we cannot see it literally, only in a likeness or appearance. The Almighty cannot be limited to merely a physical presence. When He appears to mankind, He veils the power of His glory in an appearance and likeness so that we will not perish because of the awesomeness of His might. It is plainly stated by the prophet himself when Ezekiel says at the very beginning, "I saw visions of God." He uses the words "looked like," "appearance," "appeared to be," "figure like" repeatedly.

He closes the first chapter with the words "the appearance of the likeness of the glory of the Lord" (NIV). If a person reads the Bible carefully and with respect for its literal meaning, he will be able to learn something.

The biblical writers were not ignoramuses. Ezekiel said it was the Lord. Those who reject biblical revelation presume that there cannot be a spiritual reality, so the Bible must be a myth used to explain totally natural occurrences. Von Daniken assumes that God cannot exist as the Bible describes Him, so He must be an astronaut. But, biblical proof of historical and scientific accuracy in every verifiable instance leads one to the correct conclusion that the Word of God is correct in things that cannot be verified by our own firsthand observation.

The whole challenge posed by von Daniken's theory is really very simple. Either a person accepts God's Word as truth or he accepts von Daniken's unbelievable and unverifiable theory as truth. If man wants to reject God's

Word, then he is at liberty to do so. But what hope is left if one believes in theories that are demonstrated to be myths?

A MORE CERTAIN WORD OF HOPE!

What explanations are there for the antiquities and mysteries of the past that von Daniken claims prove his theory? Man was created in the image of God. Man is a being with intelligence and the ability to dream. He has emotions, intuitive abilities, and a need to worship. Man, created in God's image, was endowed with great capabilities that explain the great art, architecture, literature, inventions, skills, and religious monuments of ancient civilizations. Ante-diluvial man possessed great storehouses of knowledge. Some of this knowledge was transmitted to post-diluvian civilization through Noah and his sons, who lived before the flood. Some of this knowledge perished in the flood. Some knowledge was undoubtedly lost as time passed after the flood.

Evolutionary ideas, including von Daniken's, do not fit the history of man. The sudden rise of advanced civilization in the Near East during the fifth and fourth millenniums does not make sense using any of these speculative theories as a basis of understanding. True science supports the literal, biblical account.

The challenges that this new UFO religion poses are not difficult to deal with. Von Daniken has thrown out a challenge that might delude the uninformed. But by turning to the Bible we find a basis for understanding where we have come from and where we are going. We are Genesis man, created in God's image. We are to be glorified, redeemed by Jesus, living with God, and participating in all the glories that await us.

It is not by accident that Genesis is the first book of the Bible. We should use it as the foundation of our biblical view of man, and man must be carefully defined as Genesis Man, no mere evolving animal but a new creation in the image of God.[23]

We prefer to accept the Bible as an accurate record of the origin and destiny of mankind. It has passed the test of science, archaeology, history, and spiritual effectiveness repeatedly. One theologian has observed that there are 2,712 individual prophecies in the Bible. Over 2,200 have been fulfilled, literally and demonstrably! As for the authors of this book, we will pay attention to God's Word!

And we have the word of the prophets made more certain, and you will do well to pay attention to it, as to a light shining in a dark place, until the day dawns and the morning star rises in your hearts. Above all, you must understand that no prophecy of Scripture came about by the prophet's own interpretation. For prophecy never had its origin in the will of man, but men spoke from God as they were carried along by the Holy Spirit. But there were also false prophets among the people, just as there will be false teachers among you. They will secretly introduce destructive heresies, even denying the sovereign Lord who bought them — bringing swift destruction on themselves (2 Pet. 1:19-21;NIV).

Von Daniken and all those who continue to promote theories based on his ideas are willfully ignorant of biblical truth. If you have not researched what the Bible has to say about man, his origin, and destiny, are you not also being willfully ignorant of the most important truth that is available to every man? You should begin today to seek the truth of God's Word — truth that will give you a sure hope!

FOOTNOTES

[1]Clifford Wilson, Ph.D., *Gods in Chariots and Other Fantasies,* Creation Life Publishers, p.11.

[2]Jacques & Janine Vallee, *The UFO Enigma,* Ballantine, p.196.

[3]*Probe the Unknown* magazine, Spring 1974, p.19.

[4]Ancient Astronauts — UFO Special, July 1976, p.47.

[5]Ibid., p.46.

[6]Brad Steiger, *The Fellowship,* Ivy Books, p.64.

[7]Edgar Castle and Rev. B.B Thiering, editors, *Some Trust in Chariots*, Popular Library — introduction.

[8]*Chariots of the Gods? Fantasy or Fraud?* by the Bible Science Association of Canada.

[9]Robert Brow, *Christianity Today* magazine, September 15, 1972, "The Late-Date Genesis Man," p.6.

[10]Edgar Castle and Rev. B.B Thiering, editors, *Some Trust in Chariots*, Popular Library, p.64.

[11]*Chariots of the Gods? Fantasy or Fraud?* Bible Science Association of Canada.

[12]Clifford Wilson, *War of the Chariots,* Master Books, p.38.

[13]Robert Brow, *Christianity Today* magazine, September 15, 1972, "The Late-Date Genesis Man," p.7.

[14]Edgar Castle and Rev. B.B Thiering, editors, *Some Trust in Chariots*, Popular Library, p.67.

[15]Ibid., p.71.

[16]Ibid., p.84.

[17]*Chariots of the Gods? Fantasy or Fraud?* Bible Science Association of Canada.

[18]Clifford Wilson, Ph.D., *Crash Go the Chariots,* A Lancer Book, p.30.

[19]The formula used is 481.4/5280 x 1,000 million = 91.1742 million. This is an error from 93 million of about 2% (1.97%). Can you imagine the mistake in navigation that would occur if ancient astronauts were off by 2% coming from 12 light years — the distance to the 20 closest stars? One light year is the distance light will travel in one year, approximately 600,000,000,000 miles! This could produce an error in navigation of over 11,820,000,000 miles. This is a distance over three times the distance from the sun to Pluto.

[20]*Chariots of the Gods? Fantasy or Fraud?* Bible Science Association of Canada.

[21]Ibid.

[22]Robert Brow, *Christianity Today* magazine, September 15, 1972, "The Late-Date Genesis Man," p.7.

CHAPTER SEVEN

PARANOID PLANET

WHO'S WATCHING US?

The question of life beyond planet Earth (extraterrestrial intelligences) has been debated by philosophers and scientists. The Pythagoreans touched upon the subject in the fifth century. Other Greek philosophers speculated about the possibility of life forms inhabiting other worlds, other realms. After Copernicus in the seventeenth century A.D., the debate attracted the attention not only of the philosophers, but of the newly-birthed modern scientists as well.

They wondered if there were other suns with planets like the Earth upon which life could exist. Astronomers gazed at the heavens through telescopes searching for signs "out there." Theories ran rampant and speculative scientists thought they saw canals on Mars. Were there hidden civilizations under the cloud cover of Venus? What life forms might be inhabiting the planets of our system? Are there planets circling other suns in the far reaches of the galaxies?

After more than 300 years of Earth-bound searching for extraterrestrial life through telescopes, twentieth century technology has allowed us to probe the universe in a more aggressive fashion. Rocket ships were no longer the province of Flash Gordon and Buck Rogers. The space age was born in our century. NASA sent two Viking landing vehicle missions to Mars to look for signs of primitive cellular life forms. The experiments that the Viking craft carried out didn't discover any evidence of extraterrestrial life. Today few scientists believe that any life exists on Mars. The manned Apollo missions to the moon in the 1970s also provided no information to indicate the presence of extraterrestrial life. The evolutionists gained no ground through these missions. Venus is far too hot to support life as we know it. No planet in our solar system is deemed likely to support life. Because other planets in our solar system are not compatible with life forms we can conceive of, the search has been pushed outward. Now we must look to other star systems in the hope of finding intelligent life. Secular man, without God, is lonely. There is a God shaped vacuum in the soul of every man. Nature abhors a vacuum. Disavow the existence of God, and the empty soul presents an open invitation to beings who from time immemorial have wanted to supplant God. Man may robe his outward questing in scientific garb, but at the end of the road the alien neighbor he meets is not someone he would want to welcome into his home.

Today the scientific search is carried on largely through radio astronomy. Radio astronomy is listening to and studying the characteristics of radio signals generated by both known natural sources and unexplained sources in the universe. In the case of ETIs (extraterrestrial intelligence), the researcher is looking for signals that indicate intelligent life. Large radio telescopic antennas are tuned in to those stars that are similar to our own sun. The theory is that life would more likely exist on planets circling a star like our sun.

The first such attempt was named Project Ozma and was conducted at the National Radio Astronomy Observatory during the 1960s. It focused on two stars, Epsilon Eridani and Tau Ceti. Since then several other searches technologically similar to Project Ozma have been conducted.

In 1983 one phase of the government-sponsored SETI

(Search for Extraterrestrial Intelligence) project began at Harvard's Oak Ridge Observatory. It was designed originally to scan sixty-eight percent of the sky. The first multi-channel spectrum analyzer scanned 131,072 channels. This system was upgraded in 1985 to scan 8.4 million channels. NASA (National Aeronautics and Space Agency), with Stanford University, is developing a ten to fifteen million channel spectrum analyzer. This is planned to be operational in the 1990s.

When the SETI project was operating at the Aimes Hershey Research Center in Mountain View, California, it was headed by Dr. John Billingham. Billingham said, "There is no doubt in our minds that intelligent life, far more advanced and complex than our own, is widespread in outer space. The United States wants to be the first nation to make contact. When we make contact it will be the biggest breakthrough in the history of mankind. These advanced civilizations could help us conquer problems like disease, pollution, food and energy shortages and natural disasters." Please remember that SETI is an ongoing U.S. Government project, funded with your tax dollars.

In spite of the lack of any evidence that ETIs exist, as conceived by the scientists, there are attempts not only to locate but to communicate with them. SETI is an attempt to establish two-way communication. The Pioneer 10 and 11 spacecraft each bear an engraved plate with symbols that are designed to indicate to any aliens that find them drifting in space that man is open to communication with the ETIs. Voyagers 1 and 2 each carry an elaborate recorded message of words and music for the same purpose. These spacecraft are all heading for interstellar space.

KNOCK, KNOCK ... WHO'S THERE?

There are some scientists who warn against attempting to communicate with ETIs. They fear that aliens could have hostile intentions. If we get their attention, they might invade planet Earth and enslave or destroy us all. The warning is too late; the invasion has already begun.

The final abolition of mankind is well-planned by the deceivers. I can assure you that ultimately they cannot win. God has definite plans for this planet revealed through the prophets of Holy Writ. Only the prophecies of the Bible are absolutely unerring in accuracy.

All psychic systems of prophecy can only hope for a small percentage of correct predictions. We assure you that you do not need a psychic bag of tricks to help or guide you. Through prayer you can go directly to the Almighty Creator of the Universe. His Word and His Spirit will be your guide through troubled and confusing times. "Ye are of God, little children, and have overcome them: because greater is he that is in you, than he that is in the world" (1 John 4:4).

Yes, the warning is too late for the masses of humanity. The aliens are here. They have been here for about 6,000 years. Now in the end of this age, as we come near to the return of Jesus Christ, they are stepping up their activities. The warning comes tardy, for UFO contactees have already communicated with the aliens. A number of them are eager to share their experience and message with the rest of us.

The deceivers have tailored their tactics to suit the mentality and outlook of the present world. This is the space age, so they come to us in space ships, masquerading as representatives of the "ascended masters of the hierarchy of the universe." Their message is crystal clear: In the midst of our despair they will save us. They will raise a human leader and endow him with supernormal powers that will enable him to put together a New World order, and from this the beneficence of world peace will proceed. Antichrist! The beast of the Apocalypse! After all, everyone wants peace don't we? Yes, we do, but we want to know who is promoting that peace and what is their actual agenda. The Bible speaks to this in some significant passages:

The disciples asked Jesus, "What shall be the sign of thy coming and of the end of the age?" In His reply Jesus said, "There shall be wars and rumors of wars...For nation shall arise against nation and kingdom against kingdom" (Matt. 24:6,7).

"There is no peace, saith my God, to the wicked" (Isa. 57:21). Daniel prophesies about the coming world ruler, the Antichrist: "And through his policy also he shall cause craft to prosper in his hand and he shall magnify himself in his heart, and by peace shall destroy many: he shall also stand up against the Prince of princes; but he shall be broken without hand" (Dan. 8:25).

"For when they shall say, Peace and safety; then sudden destruction cometh upon them, as travail upon a woman with child; and they shall not escape" (1 Thess. 5:3).

In Revelation John writes about the works of the false prophet. The second beast, the false prophet, is the religious counterpart of the political antichrist:

"And deceiveth them that dwell on the earth by the means of those miracles which he had power to do in the sight of the beast; saying to them that dwell on the earth, that they should make an image to the beast, which had the wound by a sword, and did live" (Rev. 13:14).

EVOLUTION IS THE LINK

Because SETI is based upon a faulty evolutionary premise and because so many of those who believe in ETIs are themselves open to the New Age metaphysics, SETI lends itself to a New Age model of reality.

A biblical model of reality will lead one to the conclusion that the extraterrestrials that people are claiming to meet through UFO encounters and trance channeling experiences are in reality evil, demonic, and hostile.

STRANGER THAN SCIENCE FICTION

How do SETI projects command such attention and respect, to the extent that they get abundant financial support from our own government as well as private foundations and other sources? SETI certainly represents a great expenditure of time and resources. We must conclude that the evolutionary bias of a majority in scientific academia contributes in no small way to this acceptance and funding of projects.

George Bernard Shaw was right about Darwin's theories! Mankind longed for a theory with scientific credibility that would allow him to throw off the yoke of God's dominion. Von Daniken represents a climax to Darwinian rationale. Darwin allowed men to scrap their ideas about man and his origin. Von Daniken offers a way to scrap biblical ideas about God and His purposes.

In the new paradigm, man is either a product of blind evolution or the result of alien genetic tampering in Earth's early ages. In this bizarre world of weird science, God is seen as early man's mythological explanation of alien visitations and contacts. The same mentality that leads one to accept an origin of life apart from the Creator also leads to the unsupported conclusion that other intelligent life forms must have evolved on other worlds.

In the political arena, the witness of former president Jimmy Carter must be noted. Carter not only saw a UFO and believed in UFOs, but he caused funding for Project SETI to be appropriated in the late 1970s. This kind of research is ongoing to this day, still funded with our tax dollars in various programs.

Astronauts Gorden Cooper, Eugene Cernan, John Young, and Edgar Mitchell have all expressed belief in ETIs and UFOs. Young speculated about life on other worlds:

> *There are so many stars that it's mathematically improbable there are no other life sources in the universe.*[1]

Young's assumption is in line with a macro evolutionary philosophy. There is no real proof of evolving ETIs or civilizations elsewhere in the universe. The mathematical probabilities are against Young's hypothesis. Evolution of life is mathematically improbable! In spite of this, the weight that our techno-evolutionary society gives such statements by scientists and other personalities creates an almost universal acceptance. Astronaut Gordon Cooper said,

Intelligent Beings from other planets regularly visit our world to enter into contact with us. [2]

It is really strange that intelligent people can accept this idea. To do so one must make an illogical leap from an unproven assumption into the black hole of end-time delusion.

UFOS, A NON-BIBLICAL FAITH SYSTEM

Many in the scientific community believe in ETIs and UFOs. Like general macro evolution, it cannot be proven, so it must be accepted by faith. One New Age author cites statements made by individuals in the scientific world:

"Many scientists now believe that extraterrestrial life exists, perhaps hundreds or even thousands of civilizations" (Bernard Oliver of Hewlett-Packard, who works with NASA); "The time will have to come when we realize that we're not the center of the universe. The galaxy may be teeming with life. There may be millions of civilizations" (Astronomer Richard Terrile of the Jet Propulsion Laboratory); and "A suitable habitat for life and a mechanism for its origin may exist near many of the billions of stars in our galaxy" (Paul Horowitz, professor of physics at Harvard University). [3]

There is a built-in prejudice against the biblical world-view among those in the humanistic educational system. While some highly-educated people are more inclined toward a completely materialistic world-view, others have sought for innovative ways to fit their humanist ideas in with the new metaphysics that touts the divinity of the human person. The New Age proclaims that one does not find God in the biblical redemptive sense. Instead, one finds God within his own soul. By descending into the depths of the human psyche, one finds his deity and is "Christed." Evolution of other life forms seems logical to a person whose university studies had led him down the garden path of pseudo-scientific delusion. Of course there are very notable exceptions. Some leading scientists such as Lambert Dolphin (Stanford Research Institute), Dr. Clifford Burdick, Dr. Nancy Kerr Del Grande (Lawrence Livermore Laboratories), Dr. Ronald Cooper (formerly with Lawrence Livermore), Dr. A. E. Wilder Smith, Dr. Duane Gish, Dr. John Morris, and a host of others are all men and women highly respected for their work in various scientific disciplines. They also are page one Genesis creationists. Each of them has done extensive scientific research in the question of origins. These people have read the evolutionists such as Darwin, Lyell, Simpson, and so on. It is a peculiar thing to consider that hardly an evolutionist can be found who has even casually read any of the scientific creationist works. What do they fear? They hurl diatribes against us, but few have read the Bible or any of the serious creation literature that is available. The works on scientific creationism are extensive and easily obtained. Who is broad-minded and who is narrow-minded? It is not difficult to form a conclusion on that matter!

There are also some research scientists who are honestly looking for scientific facts and who do not allow their leaning toward an evolutionary world-view to color their work. Therefore, we cannot criticize the entire scientific community. As the old saying goes, "Don't paint them all with the same brush." However, there is a disturbing trend toward the metaphysical as those who start from an evolutionary paradigm proceed to move into a New Age perception of reality.

Many scientists who believe in ETIs also believe in UFOs and have taken a step beyond science, a step that places the UFO believer into a new religious faith. It is one thing to believe in the possible existence of other life forms. It is an entirely different matter to believe aliens from other worlds are now communicating with people in our world. Inevitably people who believe the UFO phenomenon to be an encounter with highly-evolved life forms will also find it easy to believe the message they proclaim. The message does not come from the ascended masters of the hierarchy. It comes from the descended lords of the abyss, the deceivers. These are days of prophetic fulfillment. Whose prophecy will you believe?

The "Tomorrow Show" hosted by Tom Snyder featured an interview with a physicist. The program on the topic of UFOs was aired in the early 1990s. The same program featured Betty Hill who was allegedly kidnaped by the crew of a flying saucer. Her story appears elsewhere in this book. The physicist discussed a 1973 Gallup Poll that showed that most Americans believe in UFOs. Also, most scientists and engineers believe in them. Of the scientists and engineers polled, eight percent believe they have seen a UFO; four percent believe they might have seen a UFO. One conclusion drawn from this poll was that the higher the educational level of a person, the more likely a person is to believe in UFOs.

The next step in the deception that is perpetrated through pseudo-science could be "scientific" verification of UFO alien contacts. As we will observe later, contactees, those who have had face to face encounters with aliens, are almost without exception involved in New Age or occultic practices like those forbidden in the Bible. (We are saying "almost" without exception to give the benefit of the doubt, but our own research points to this as a universal fact.)

The *Spiritual Counterfeits Journal* noted,

> *A 1973 Gallup Poll estimated that fifteen million Americans claim to have seen UFOs [that figure has risen to twenty million in the early 1990s] ... Twenty to thirty percent are true aerial phenomena that cannot be accounted for ... There are, by conservative estimate, over 2,000 cases of human encounters with landed UFOs and their occupants, and some 700 instances where physical evidence has been left behind [again the numbers had risen dramatically by the early 1990s.]* [4]

In the same issue they continued,

> *An authoritative, and possibly conservative, estimate is that there are 50,000 silent contactees in the United States alone.* [5]

The number of contactees has risen dramatically in the last few years along with the increase in New Age and occult practices. We are seeing a parallel rise in both New Age and UFO phenomena. A New Age writer who practices trance channeling says,

> *Very often UFO contactees are, by their own admission, individuals who have become disillusioned with the existing religious institutions. (In the Western world probably Judaism or Christianity).* [6]

Often we have observed that UFO contactees have rejected biblical faith to turn to a new metaphysical faith based on Eastern mysticism. This would include all occultic, Luciferic, or New Age cults and religions. How long will it be before UFOs are "proven" to exist by scientists with New Age leanings?

OUTER SPACE — SPACED OUT!

Former astronaut Edgar Mitchell served as lunar module pilot in the Apollo program. He and commander Alan Shepard spent more than thirty hours on the lunar surface, including nine hours of moon walks. It is interesting that Mitchell did extrasensory perception experiments while in lunar orbit. After resigning from the Navy and NASA in 1972, he became chairman of the Institute of Noetic Sciences in Palo Alto, California. He is now president of the Edgar D. Mitchell Corporation in Washington, DC. Wanda Marrs writes,

> *Former NASA scientist and astronaut, Mitchell now heads up a New Age organization, the Institute of Homus Noeticus, to promote the New Age "God-man" concept.* [7]

Reports claiming that there is an underlying belief in NASA in the concept of UFOs and ETIs are probably accurate. It is said that they are looking forward to ETI contact in the hope that we will gain advanced technologies through such encounters with alien civilizations.

...NASA believes that any intelligent life that would contact us would have solved their problems and most likely would have transcended the laws of physics as well, dashing about the universe at the speed of light (or faster). [8]

Thus we observe that there are those in the scientific realm who believe in ETIs and UFOs. Even NASA has gotten involved to some extent in the UFO drama. Any scientist who gets involved with alien contacts could be opening himself up to alien deceiver influence or infestation.

THE MEN FROM FOGGY BOTTOM (WASHINGTON, DC)

The mind set of politicians has a lot to do with the funding made available to projects like SETI and OZMA. We would like to believe that our politicians are spending our money on worthwhile projects. One cannot be sure ... Most politicians vote funding into the budget for two reasons. First is the consideration, "Will this get me reelected?" Second, they vote according to their world-view. *UFO* magazine referred to Jimmy Carter's speech to NICAP (National Investigative Committee on Aerial Phenomenon):

Carter said that his sighting took place around 7:15 P.M. one October night in 1969. The UFO was a sharply outlined, luminous globe "about the same size as the moon, maybe a little smaller." [9]

Carter is not the only high-ranking politician who has expressed belief in UFOs or the paranormal. Senator Claiborne Pell is probably one of the most prominent New Age advocates on the political scene today.

Perhaps the most avid, some would say fanatical, New Ager in Congress, Pell, a Democrat from Rhode Island, is chairman of the powerful Senate Foreign Relations Committee. He is a vocal advocate of psychic research and according to *U.S. News & World Report,* his bookcase in his private capitol office is crammed with occult books such as *The Astral Body,* which examines out-of-body experiences.

Pell, who admits he frequents spirit mediums, has befriended such New Age notables as psychic magician Uri Geller and the late Theosophy/Hindu philosopher Krishnamurti, who once was thought to be the New Age "christ."[10]

Because politicians tend to reflect what is going on among their constituency, we can plausibly assume that the interest in UFOs, ETIs, and other New Age ideas has increased in Washington as it has in general. This increase will undoubtedly be reflected in increasing funds for SETI-styled projects. It seems likely that there will one day be official recognition of contact with aliens. We fully expect this to happen.

It is not difficult to construct a plausible scenario of a future time, in which the world's governments make contact with ETIs ... and receive instructions on how to conduct the affairs of our planet. [11]

This scenario fits the biblical prophecies about the end of this age, many of which deal with end-time delusion and deception. When Jesus was about to give His most extensive prophetic teaching, the Olivet Discourse, He prefaced His remarks by warning, "Take heed that no man deceive you" (Matt. 24:4). Saint Paul warned of "doctrines of devils" leading men astray in the "latter times." Satan is called the deceiver. The second letter of Paul to the church at Thessalonica in Greece describes certain aspects of the coming Antichrist, "the man of sin, the son of perdition." Paul says that he comes with "lying signs and wonders and all deceivableness of unrighteousness in them that perish..." Because they forsake His Word, God himself will send "strong delusion that they should believe a lie." In the Greek text "a lie" actually reads, "THE lie." What is "the lie?" That man can be God. That is the basis on which the man of sin will demand worship since he will be the satanically (alien?) appointed world ruler and focal point of humanity's self-worship. (Read 2 Thess. 2:1-17 for the entire context.)

Government leaders will eventually get involved with the deceivers (ETIs). This is portrayed in various passages in the Book of Revelation. For example, Revelation 13:2b depicts the Beast, the Antichrist, as getting his power and authority from the alien dragon that is revealed as none other than Satan himself. (See Rev. 12:9.)

In a time when intense problems are crushing in on our world, it may be with the best of intentions that leaders could seek alien help. The Antichrist will not come as an ogre. He will come with diplomacy and great personal charisma. He is the master of the deceivers. He will come as an "angel of light." He offers to solve the problems no one else has been able to master. He will, in short, be attractive, not repulsive.

When we come to Revelation 16, we see a major maneuver of the deceivers (ETIs) in the Great Tribulation. The seven years of Earth's worst agonies are about to climax in the battle of Armageddon. John, writer of the Apocalypse, tells us this:

And blasphemed the God of heaven because of their pains and their sores, and repented not of their deeds. And the sixth angel poured out his vial upon the great river Euphrates; and the water thereof was dried up, that the way of the kings of the east might be prepared.

And I saw three unclean spirits like frogs come out of the mouth of the dragon, and out of the mouth of the beast, and out of the mouth of the false prophet (Rev. 16:11-13).

Notice that the unclean spirits are entities from the

supernatural or paranormal realm. They are not frogs, but they are "like frogs." This indicates their alien appearance. They will probably look humanoid except for their frog-like features. They go forth to deceive the political rulers of Earth. They travel, meet people, have conferences and discussions. There are planning sessions. Earth must get ready for a hostile alien invasion. The idea that Jesus is going to come back and establish a kingdom must now be dealt with once and for all. It is not Jesus, they will say, but a leader of interplanetary warlike beings who are coming to conquer Earth. Representing themselves in New Age terminology, these "ascended masters of the hierarchy of the universe" will offer assistance to prepare for the coming war. The situation will be even worse then. Antichrist has sporadic uprisings against him throughout the Tribulation, especially in the last three and one-half years. At Armageddon the nations are not united. They come to make war among themselves and against Israel. Only when Jesus and the glorified Church in His entourage appear will they unite to confront Him as a common enemy. You will note an element of conjecture in this paragraph. Understand, the authors of this book believe this is accurate. Revelation further reveals the following:

For they are the spirits of devils, working miracles, which go forth unto the kings of the earth and of the whole world, to gather them to the battle of that great day of God Almighty. Behold, I come as a thief. Blessed is he that watcheth, and keepeth his garments, lest he walk naked, and they see his shame. And he gathered them together into a place called in the Hebrew tongue Armageddon (Rev. 16:14-16).

When government leaders get involved in SETI, they give credibility to the deceivers who are now manifesting their presence in a limited way, compared to what is to come. I talked to the famed Washington, DC psychic Jeanne Dixon. She said that the UFO people would soon be making contact with the governments of America and other countries. She has claimed to be in psychic communication with the UFO astronauts. The UFO delusion will provide a power base for the coming Antichrist. We are seeing the stage set. How long will it be before a man possessed by the master of the deceivers walks on stage to declare a one-world government?

STAR-GAZING FOR THE MAN ON THE STREET

There is a longing today for science fiction to become a reality. It has become a new religion for many secular people. They receive it by faith. This is reflected in the popularity of science fiction magazines, books, movies, and television productions. Each technological breakthrough in space travel is greeted with mass enthusiasm.

When we entered the race to reach the moon, the media reminded us of the works of science-fiction author Jules Verne who wrote *From the Earth to the Moon*. As manned space missions became common, one of the first modern books and movies that captured readers' attention and imagination was Arthur C. Clarke's *2001: A Space Odyssey*. His work was seen by millions of people, many of whom accept his New Age world-view wholeheartedly. "Star Trek" was one of the most popular television series in the 1960s — particularly after it was cancelled by the network and put into syndicated re-runs. We are still treated to continuous repeats of the original "Star Trek" series. The *Star Trek* movies have packed the theaters. The new series, "Star Trek: the Next Generation" promises to play on for quite some time. It is a veritable course in evolution, paranormal phenomena, involvement with extra-terrestrials, and life on other worlds. It is a New Age feast, dressed up in the trappings of science on the periphery.

"George Lucas. Movie director and producer of the *Star Wars* saga, *Willow*, and other New Age-oriented movies ... He has teamed up with actor Ron Howard, formerly of the 'Andy Griffith Show,' to produce New Age cinemas. "[12]

Science fiction serves as a conduit providing a free flow of New Age ideas and Aquarian revelations. Science fiction provides a rationale for the new pseudo-science that seeks to investigate and validate New Age phenomena, including the SETI delusion.

"Today, with the emergence of the so-called New Consciousness, science fiction finds itself at the synapse between the old mythology of technological idealism and a new mythology based on scientific validation of paranormal phenomena." [13]

Serious scientific investigation of the UFO phenomena is also ongoing at the present! How long will it be before some researcher claims to have proof for the existence of UFOs and ETIs? These New Age scientists will mix Eastern mystical religion with establishment science to create an illusion of reality. Brad Steiger, a New Age writer, refers to "a blending of technology and traditional religious concepts." [14]

The average citizen does not realize that a techno-occultic bill of goods is being sold to the public by some scientists, politicians, and entertainment personalities. The man on the street is gazing at the stars because he is being told by so many different "authorities" that not only is man evolving, but that there are other evolving civilizations more advanced than ours, and that some day we will be friends and partners with these aliens in a grand adventure in an upward process of evolution leading to God-hood!

ASSUMPTIONS, NOT PROOF

The basis of this scientific effort to locate or contact alien intelligences is in error. The assumptions underlying it are false. The evidence for it is non-existent. The prospect of wasted time and resources is enormous. The danger of deception is grave.

In the first place, it assumes the existence of extraterrestrial beings for which there is no hard evidence whatsoever.

In the second place ... "If only one UFO is to visit the

earth each year, we can calculate what mean launch rate is required at each of these million worlds. The number turns out to be 10,000 launches per year per civilization..." The author then comments, tongue in cheek, that "this seems excessive."

In the third place, the extraterrestrial theory draws conclusions of a profoundly "spiritual" nature while conveniently avoiding that controversial label. Entities that operate with total disregard for the inviolate laws of physics, traveling at the speed of light or faster and having "solved all their problems," would have to be classified as "spiritual," semantic arguments notwithstanding.[15]

Charles Darwin, Erich von Daniken, Arthur Clarke, Carl Sagan, Isaac Asimov, and a host of others have laid a mythical foundation for the present research directed toward locating ETIs and establishing communication with the aliens. Seeing our day, Paul wrote,

For the time will come when men will not put up with sound doctrine. Instead, to suit their own desires, they will gather around them a great number of teachers to say what their itching ears want to hear. They will turn their ears away from the truth and turn aside to myths (2 Tim. 4:3,4;NIV).

Thinking of the Antichrist in the coming tribulation time, songwriter Larry Norman penned these words:

In the midst of a war he offered us peace
He came like a lover from out of the east
With the face of an angel and the heart of a beast
His intentions were six sixty six
He walked up to the temple with gold in his hand
And bought off the priests and propositioned the land
And the world was his harlot and laid in the sand
While the band played six sixty six
We served at his table and slept on the floor
Then he starved us and beat us and nailed us to the door

Well I'm ready to die, I can't take any more
and I'm sick of his lies and his tricks.
He told us he loved us but that was a lie
There was blood in his pocket and death in his eye
Well my number is up and I'm weary to die
If the band will play six sixty six.

FOOTNOTES

[1]*Midnight* magazine, "UFOs Really Exist," 12/30/74.

[2]UFO Education Center bulletin 10/21/76.

[3]Ruth Montgomery, *Aliens Among Us,* Fawcett/Crest, p.5.

[4]*SCP Journal,* August 1977, Vol.1 No.2, "UFOs — Is Science Fiction Coming True?" p. 14.

[5]Ibid., p.17.

[6]Brad Steiger, *The Fellowship,* Ivy Books, p.39.

[7]Wanda Marrs, *New Age Lies to Women,* Living Truth Publications, p.43.

[8]*SCP Journal,* August 1977, Vol.1 No.2, "UFOs — Is Science Fiction Coming True?" p.16.

[9]*UFO* magazine, M. J. Ernst, "President Carter Launches New UFO Study to Probe Air Force Cover-up," April 1978, p.30.

[10]Wanda Marrs, *New Age Lies to Women,* Living Truth Publications, p.41.

[11]*SCP Journal,* August 1977, Vol.1 No.2, "The Modern Prometheus: Science Fiction and the New Consciousness," p.8.

[12]Wanda Marrs, *New Age Lies to Women,* Living Truth Publications, p.44.

[13]*SCP Journal,* August 1977, Vol.1 No.2, "The Modern Prometheus: Science Fiction and the New Consciousness," p.3.

[14]Brad Steiger, *The Fellowship,* Ivy Books, p.2.

[15]*SCP Journal,* August 1977, Vol.1 No.2, "UFOs — Is Science Fiction Coming True?" p.16-17.

CHAPTER EIGHT

UFOs AND THE PARANORMAL

SPIRITUAL FORCES — SOLID OBJECTS

We are dealing with a mysterious phenomenon in UFOs and ETIs. There are some baffling aspects that need to be set in the context of an over-all picture if we are to maintain our perspective. The thesis of this book is that there is a reality to the UFO experience. We believe that some UFOs which cannot be explained by natural causes may better be explained by spiritual realities.

UFOs ARE SPIRITUAL, NOT MATERIAL

It is no longer reasonable to deny the reality of UFOs. What we must do is to discover evidence that will lead us to a correct conclusion as to their nature, origin, and purpose. If millions of people worldwide have encountered UFOs and many have encountered alien beings, then it is important that we present an explanation for UFOs and also a plan of action for dealing with the growing numbers of people who are being affected by UFOs.

It was estimated over fifteen years ago that tens of thousands of people had direct contact with ETIs, in the U.S.A. alone. This number is most certainly larger today:

> . . . there is a growing army of those who claim to
> have had actual contact with UFO occupants. An

authoritative, and possibly conservative, estimate is that there are 50,000 silent contactees in the United States alone.[1]

So we are not dealing with only a kooky minority. A significant segment of our society needs help. The UFO, flying-saucer scheme is not new. In past times in our history they were not called flying saucers, but they manifested themselves in other guises. One author makes this observation:

A historical survey reveals that reports of strange objects in the skies are laced through documents of the ancient and recent past. Interestingly, the records seem to indicate that UFOs have adapted themselves to the cultural milieu and the technological capacities of the observers.[2]

Noted UFO researcher Jacques Vallee writes,

...UFOs are paranormal in nature and a modern space age manifestation of phenomenon that assumes different guises in different historical contexts.[3]

Because they are now appearing in a new, modern guise should tell us something about their purposes. Man was not so ignorant in the past that he could not accurately describe a "flying saucer." Rather, the "flying saucers" appeared in different forms in the past. The fact that they have appeared in different forms over the centuries reveals their purpose: deceiving men in the historical context of the day in which they appeared. Real aliens from a far-away world would not need to trick people by appearing in different guises. Deceptive demonic entities would certainly do this! J. Allen Hynek and Jacques Vallee write,

If UFOs are, indeed, somebody else's "nuts and bolts hardware," then we must still explain how such tangible hardware can change shape before our eyes, vanish in a Cheshire cat manner (not even leaving a

grin), seemingly melt away in front of us, or apparently "materialize" mysteriously before us without apparent detection by persons nearby or in neighboring towns. We must wonder, too, where UFOs are "hiding" when not manifesting themselves to human eyes.[4]

If they are not material, then what other option is left to us? We will look at evidence shortly that points to the spiritual nature of UFOs.

A METHOD OF PROGRAMMING MAN

Disturbing effects of the UFO phenomenon are the changes in the perceptions of reality that so often occur to people who have had encounters with them, especially those who have face-to-face encounters with the UFO entities. The whole UFO event appears to have the purpose of conditioning, even brainwashing people. Jacques Vallee explained when interviewed:

> **Hastings:** ...*maybe it is a deliberate attempt to influence us by doing things that will call attention to anomalies ... non-realities...*
>
> **Vallee:** *I said I thought it was a control system, a way to condition our social behavior.*[5]

The fact that UFOs call attention to "non-realities" to control or "condition" people demonstrates that they are playing tricks and mind-games. They are lying to us!

The evidence of this manipulation is apparent to all who honestly research the phenomenon. Vallee records the following:

> *Perhaps the most important effects from the UFO technology are the social ones and not the physical ones. In other words the physical reality may serve only as a kind of triggering device to provide images for the witnesses to report. These perceptions are manipulated to create certain kinds of social effects.*[6]

The UFOs are serving the purpose of social engineering.

In other words, they are causing a shift in the perception of mankind, a change in the world-view of society. Physical effects, the physical evidence left at some UFO sightings, serve only as a deceptive proof of the world-view that the entities connected with the UFO phenomenon want mankind to accept. This is the biggest con-game ever pulled on humanity.

We are going to explore the mechanism UFOs use to provide apparent material proof of their existence. We will look at evidence that points to their spiritual nature. It is important to realize that in dealing with this phenomenon, the senses and perceptions of witnesses must be critically evaluated. The UFO contactee may not be the best witness because of his subjective feelings that may have been manipulated to such an extent that he can no longer judge between real physical experiences and hallucinatory images.

We have evidence that the phenomenon can create a distortion of the sense of reality or to substitute artificial sensations for the real ones.[7]

A DEFINITE SPIRITUAL OVERTONE

One thing that points to the spiritual nature of UFOs is the use of spiritual themes that are so much a part of their activities. We must deal not only with ideas such as the origin of man and the meaning of life. The UFOs themselves exhibit characteristics that are more spiritual in nature than physical. The fact that UFOs generate a physical effect does not prove them to be physical in make-up. Rather, it proves that spiritual beings can manipulate physical reality. Again we note what Vallee writes:

...no theory of their origin and nature can be constructed without reference to theories of the origin of man and the nature of life.[8]

Another researcher observes,

...the extraterrestrial theory draws conclusions of a

profoundly "spiritual" nature while conveniently avoiding that controversial label. Entities that operate with total disregard for the inviolate laws of physics, travelling at the speed of light or faster and having "solved all their problems," would have to be classified as "spiritual," semantic arguments notwithstanding.[9]

We will also observe in other chapters the spiritual messages UFO deceivers have consistently shared with those who have had face-to-face contact. This is perhaps the most convincing evidence of all. It is interesting that they twist or deny many important biblical truths. Why would supposedly evolved intelligences from other worlds be so concerned about a local, unique, religious manifestation? They should not be threatened by something we would eventually "outgrow" as a race. The obvious answer is that the Bible makes their attempt to deceive us obvious. It thwarts their plans for mass brainwashing and takeover. They must deny the truth of the Bible.

A SHIFT IN PERCEPTIONS

A definite program is ongoing to shift our perceptions as a race. Because of the years of sightings, face-to-face encounters, and other on-the-scene evidence left behind the appearances of UFOs, people are no longer deriding the UFO idea. This new belief is being created by reinforcement and repetition. Mankind is being brainwashed by UFOs and other related phenomena to deny the biblical concepts concerning our origin and destiny. Vallee notes that UFOs have moved man toward a new world-view:

A majority of the public and practically every scientist has thought UFOs were nonsense—and that is why there are few UFO detectives. Now things are changing. So many people have seen strange phenomena that a new belief has been born ... Unfortunately, once disturbed from its comfortable position of rest, the public will shift to the other extreme and start believing in space visitations.[10]

SPIRITUAL ENTITIES WITH PHYSICAL EFFECTS

We have noted that UFO contactees or advocates may have perceptions that are not accurate. People who have accepted the deception will not be able to discern the reality behind the facade. In spite of this it is noteworthy to observe their doubts. One New Age author presents an interesting theory:

I have even come to suspect that, in some instances, what we have been terming "spaceships" may actually be a form of higher intelligence rather than vehicles transporting occupants.[11]

He goes on to observe that the telepathic influence of UFO beings gives them the ability to directly imprint certain images on the minds of those in contact with them.

I feel, too, that these intelligences have the ability to influence the human mind telepathically in order to project what appear to be three dimensional images to the witnesses of UFO activity.[12]

We note this because certainly the deceptive ability of these beings to influence the perception of reality of the contactee is an important element in the whole UFO phenomenon. Jacques Vallee is not any sort of fundamentalist Christian. We cite him frequently because of his independent, scientific point of view:

...the phenomenon has the ability to create a distortion of the sense of reality or to substitute artificial sensations for the real ones.[13]

A spiritual entity causing direct manipulation of perceptions does not answer every aspect of the UFOs. There is too much direct physical evidence that has been observed to explain all of it through direct manipulation of images in the mind of the contactee. A physicist tells us that,

> *Physicist James McCampbell, speaking to a UFO symposium in 1975, rendered a succinct analysis of the problems encountered in a scientific study of UFO characteristics: "Evidence left at landing sites leaves little room for doubt that UFOs are heavy, ponderous objects when at rest. Yet in flight, their startling departures, sudden stops, and right angle turns at high speed require them to be virtually massless."* [14]

He brings up a very difficult issue. There is obvious physical evidence that indicates an object with apparent mass. Then, on the other hand, there is evidence that denies the laws of physics or demands an object with no mass at all.

What kind of evidence is there in the UFO phenomenon? Let us look at it and attempt to classify it by two categories: direct manipulation of the minds of contactees and direct manipulation of energy fields. Mind manipulation can explain many direct contact experiences. Energy field manipulation can explain many visual, auditory, and physical effects. The following chart gives the major categories of effects that UFOs have been observed to create.

McCampbell compiled the following chart:

PERFORMANCE
Levitation
Extreme Acceleration and Deceleration
Nearly Right-angle Turns
Absence of Sonic Booms
Propulsion
ATMOSPHERIC EFFECTS
Surrounding Clouds
Colored Halos (change with acceleration)
Dazzling Brightness
Luminous Tails and Lingering "Clouds"

LANDING SITES
Pungent Odors
Baked Earth
Charred Organic Matter
ELECTRICAL INTERFERENCE
Internal Combustion Engines
Head Lights
Radio and Television
Power Transmission
PHYSIOLOGICAL RESPONSES
Humming Sounds
Body Heating
Paralysis
Electric Shock
Sunburn
Induced Emotions
ANIMAL REACTIONS
Fear or Panic
Paralysis[15]

Can we bring some logic to these conflicting effects? First the direct manipulation of the mind of the contactee could explain some sighting evidence in the categories of PERFORMANCE and ATMOSPHERIC EFFECTS. Perhaps some PHYSIOLOGICAL RESPONSES and ANIMAL REACTIONS could also be explained by mind manipulation.

However, energy field manipulation could explain some of these same things. For example, all the PERFORMANCE effects observed through sightings may be the observation of concentrated energy fields giving an appearance of mass. ATMOSPHERIC EFFECTS may also be explained in this way. LANDING SITES are probably the effects of matter and energy manipulation as are the ELECTRICAL INTERFERENCE effects. These two categories contain evidence of a nature that indicates an actual physical effect. Energy fields affecting material objects could conceivably cause charring and broken objects such as trees. Certain PHYSIOLOGICAL RESPONSES—such as humming sounds, paralysis, electric shock, and sunburn — may also be the result of energy field manipulation. Vallee notes that the effects created by UFOs are a combination of phenomena:

It is conceivable that there is one phenomenon that is visual and another that creates the physical traces. What I am saying is that a strange kind of deception may be involved.[16]

Is it conceivable that spiritual entities can create such effects? We believe that given the biblical record of angelic activities, it is entirely reasonable to believe that fallen angels could manipulate energy fields to produce many of these effects. Other effects could be accomplished by direct deceptive manipulation of the minds of contactees by these evil spirits. This indicates demonic deception involving illusions.

THE PARANORMAL REALM

Many observers of unexplained and paranormal events have noticed a parallel between the paranormal occurrences and the UFO activities. J. Allen Hynek, a scientist and UFO investigator, noted that,

...we should consider the various factors that strongly suggest a linkage, or at least a parallelism with occurrences of a paranormal nature.[17]

He goes on to note the ability of UFOs to dematerialize or change shape:

Another peculiarity is the alleged ability of certain UFOs to dematerialize ... There are quite a few reported instances where two distinctly different UFOs hovering in a clear sky will converge and eventually merge into one object. These are the types of psychic phenomena that are confronting us in the UFO mystery.[18]

Professor Hynek came to the conclusion that UFOs are probably paranormal. In biblical terminology we would say that they are spiritual entities, demons.

Many UFO reports, he said, seem to pertain more to accounts of "poltergeists"(cases where objects fly around the room and strange sounds are heard)and other types of "psychic" manifestations than to "actual solid items of nuts and bolts hardware.""This is one of the reasons," added Dr. Hynek, "why I cannot accept the obvious explanation of UFOs as visitors from outer space"[19]

How do we explain the ability of spiritual entities to manipulate the physical realm? Let us take a trip to Flatland.

FLATLAND

Edwin Abbot wrote *Flatland* in 1884. The theme of this book is an examination of how a three-dimensional being would relate to people in a two-dimensional world. If we were to step into such a world, only a small portion of our body could interact with it at any one time. As we moved in their world, our appearance to the "Flatlanders" would constantly change in shape and size. We could disappear merely by stepping out of the plane of their world. We could just as suddenly reappear. If we were to pass a ball through this world, it would appear at first as a small circle, getting larger, then smaller, then disappearing. A cube on edge or other less uniform objects would also change shape and size as they passed through.

Using this analogy, let us suppose that spiritual beings are on another, higher dimension from humankind. They would have similar effects upon our world as we would have on Flatland. If they are able to manipulate energy, to give it a concentration, then they could cause this energy concentration to take different shapes and sizes to generate an appearance of solid objects.

An example of this energy effect is a prank one of the

authors (R.L.S.) pulled with some fellow sailors in the U.S. navy while working in an electronics shop. One night, through boredom, he decided to hook up a voltage circuit to create a Jacob's Ladder. These may be seen in the old sci-fi movies where electricity climbs upward between two metallic rods. He hooked several hundred volts up to a transformer to boost it at a ratio of 10,000 to one. What he ended up with were several hundreds of thousands of volts. This was high voltage, low amperage energy, so it was relatively, though not entirely, safe. When he turned on the circuit in the darkened room, there were visible sheets of blue energy glowing between the metal legs and sides of the work benches! The energy appeared almost solid in the dark. This shows that it is possible that concentrated energy can at times appear to be solid given the right conditions. Such energy would no doubt also cause interference with electrical circuits of every kind, which would explain many effects that UFOs can generate. This could also be why UFOs appear more frequently at night than in the daytime. Energy fields would probably be somewhat transparent. A darkened background would make them appear to be more solid.

Consider what a physicist and specialist in relativity theory noted:

> *Drawing from what we know can happen in seances and poltergeist activity, it seems that these supernatural forces can manipulate matter and energy, extracting energy from the atmosphere, for example (which manifests as a local temperature change), to manipulate matter and produce an apparent violation of the second law [of thermodynamics], and I guess my feeling is that on a larger scale this is what a UFO could be. I'm not saying I know that it is, but only that it could be. It seems to me likely that UFOs are large-scale violations of the second law in which energy is arranged to take on enough of a force field appearance so that it appears to look like matter, yet it's really just energy*

concentration — it's not really solid matter in the usual sense. [20]

The point to all of this is that a spiritual explanation fits entirely with the UFO effects. Beings from a higher dimensional plane than our own, who are able to manipulate energy, could generate an appearance of mass, speed, and physical effects. Given the ability of deceptive manipulation of the minds of people, they could also give an impression of alien entities, actual physical contact, and what their ships look like on the inside. The ability of Satan to manipulate the minds of people, especially those who reject the Creator, is documented not only in the Bible, but in actual case histories. This is why we have come to the firm conclusion that UFOs are manifestations of deceptive spiritual beings.

UFOs POSE A REAL THREAT TO MEN

The UFO phenomena are manifestations of living beings that are here to deceive mankind. They appear in their UFO form because they wish to change our perception of reality. That they are alive rather than mechanical is not only our conclusion. One researcher noted this:

John Keel, one of the most respected researchers in this field, noted that "over and over again, witnesses have told me in hushed tones, 'you know, I don't think that thing I saw was mechanical at all. I got the distinct impression it was alive.'" [21]

We remind you again of Vallee's observation that

UFOs and related phenomena are the means through which man's concepts are being rearranged. [22]

UFOs are changing the perceptions of mankind. They are taking over the minds and hearts of men. The danger can be seen in the progressive possession of some individual contactees that takes place over a period of time.

It seems as if an external force takes control of

people. In the close encounters people may lose their ability to move or speak; in the abduction cases, which are the most extreme example, they gradually enter into a series of experiences during which they lose control of their senses.[23]

These beings are using deception, mind manipulation, and eventually possession to control people:

Demons, as fallen angels, apparently retain great powers, such as the manipulation and restructuring of matter, as well as the ability to influence or control human consciousness and experience through classic possession by direct psychic implantation of a set of experiences.[24]

We believe UFOs can only be explained by the spiritual entity idea, rather than as aliens in spaceships. If this is true and they are here to deceive mankind, then there is a horrible reality behind what at first glance might appear to be merely strange or eccentric. There is an evil-minded intent behind UFOs that is extremely hazardous to anyone who dabbles in the realm.

We urge all who have an interest in UFOs to realize the real danger that they pose. The apostle Paul warned, "Lest Satan should get an advantage of us: for we are not ignorant of his devices" (2 Cor. 2:11).

FOOTNOTES

[1]*SCP Journal,* August 1977, Vol.1 No.2, "UFOs — Is Science Fiction Coming True?" p.17.

[2]Ibid., p.14.

3Jacques Vallee interview, "Vallee Discusses UFO Control System," *Fate Magazine,* p.61.

[4]J. Allen Hynek and Jacques Vallee, *The Edge of Reality,* Henry Regnery Company, pp.xii-xiii.

[5]Ibid., p.245.

[6]Jacques Vallee interview, "Vallee Discusses UFO Control System," *Fate Magazine,* p.65.

[7]Ibid., p.63.

[8]Jacques & Janine Vallee, *The UFO Enigma*, Ballantine, p.196.

[9]*SCP Journal*, August 1977, Vol.1 No.2, "UFOs — Is Science Fiction Coming True?" p.17.

[10]Jacques Vallee, *Messengers of Deception*, Bantaam, p.245.

[11]Brad Steiger, *The Fellowship*, Ivy Books, p.49.

[12]Ibid.

[13]Jacques Vallee interview, "Vallee Discusses UFO Control System," *Fate Magazine*, p.63.

[14]*SCP Journal*, August 1977, Vol.1 No.2, "UFOs — Is Science Fiction Coming True?" p.14.

[15]Ibid., p.15.

[16]Jacques Vallee interview, "Vallee Discusses UFO Control System," *Fate Magazine*, p.63.

[17]J. Allen Hynek interview, *UFO Report Magazine*, August 1976, p.61.

[18]Ibid.

[19]J. Allen Hynek interview, "The Unexplained Column," by Allen Spraggett, November 8, 1975.

[20]*SCP Journal*, August 1977, Vol.1 No.2, "UFOs — Is Science Fiction Coming True?" p.20. Quoting Dr. Curt Wagner, a physicist whose (Ph.D.) degree was earned in the field of general relativity theory.

[21]Ibid., p.15.

[22]Jacques Vallee interview, "Vallee Discusses UFO Control System," *Fate Magazine*, p.61.

[23]Ibid., p.64.

[24]*SCP Journal*, August 1977, Vol.1 No.2, "UFOs — Is Science Fiction Coming True?" p.19.

CHAPTER NINE

WHO GOES THERE?

FRIEND OR FOE?

CLOSE ENCOUNTERS
OF THE THIRD & FOURTH KIND

Many who believe in UFOs as real spacecraft and ETIs as highly evolved alien beings think that mankind will benefit through contact and eventual cooperation with the aliens. There is an underlying assumption that the UFO entities are benevolent. They are assumed to have our own welfare at heart. Indeed, the UFO entities themselves have been telling people the same thing. We are, according to these beings, on the threshold of an evolutionary step into a new humanity. "Homo sapiens" will evolve into "homo superiors." If we will accept their leadership, we can make this change as a race. If not, we may perish because of our own foolishness. They present themselves as the benefactors and guides of humanity.

The deceivers' activities have rooted these ideas deeply in our culture. Decades of science fiction movies and television programs have led the public to believe the lie. *2001 — A Space Odyssey* and *Star Trek*, among many others, have shifted perceptions away from the alien menace of H.G. Wells' *War of the Worlds*.

In a stunning inversion of Wells' martian invaders, Clarke and *Star Trek* have conditioned our minds to accept any consciousness greater than our own as benevolent and helpful.[1]

That statement is only partially accurate since on the other end of the spectrum some movies and television shows have brought to the screen the terror of malevolent UFO invasion. *Invasion of the Body Snatchers, Alien, Aliens,* and cinemas of similar genre have presented a horrifying picture of the aliens. However, even that serves to promote the extraterrestrial idea. The deceivers have a purpose both for the positive and negative aspects of this PR campaign concerning UFOs and ETIs. Humankind is being conditioned to accept the idea of both "good" and "bad" UFO beings. Perhaps for now, the main emphasis is on the "good."

The assumption that UFO beings exist, are visiting Earth and are primarily benevolent is dangerous. First, there is abundant proof of the evil nature of these beings. These evil agents do not reveal their true goals since they are attempting to deceive.

One writer quotes a fellow New Age advocate saying that there are evil forces involved in some UFO phenomena. He refers to Ahrimanic powers. The Ahrimanic powers are fallen angels of Persian and Chaldean tradition. These Ahrimanic beings are involved in "some" UFO encounters according to Brad Steiger:

> *The objective of the Ahrimanic powers is to pull down all humanity.*[2]

Steiger is quoting military and aviation historian Trevor James Constable. He continues to refer to Constable:

> *The struggle, as he sees it, is for the soul, rather than the planet, of man.*[3]

Neither one of these men approaches the study of this subject from a biblical point of view. In fact both promote New Age ideas. The startling thing is that they see the obvious evil intention of the deceivers. They believe that some ETIs are evil. Ominously, they, with most other UFO advocates, assume that those beings who put on a pleasant mien are not evil. This flawed assumption is a greater threat to humanity than the openly hostile intentions that are sometimes exhibited by UFO beings. If "aliens" act the part of both enemy and friend, we can conclude that they are attempting to cause us to blindly rush from an open threat into a hidden trap.

We have seen no evidence to indicate that UFO aliens are not evil — the very deceivers of the end-times.

The "evil alien" experience is a feint to push humanity into the arms of the "benevolent alien," who in reality is the greater danger. There are some very disturbing aspects of UFO encounters. They have been playing hypnotic mind games with humanity. In fact, the beings behind the UFO phenomenon are demonic powers. They are attempting to condition us to accept the New Age. They work to prepare mankind for the coming of the Antichrist. There is a real war going on in which we are involved whether we realize it or not. It is time for the Church to awaken to the threat that UFOs and the New Age present, not only for our own survival, but also for the salvation of a multitude of lost souls deceived by this and other aspects of the great lie of the end-times. New Age author Brad Steiger, quoting Constable, writes this:

> *Man will win or lose the battle for Earth itself, for he is at once the goal of the battle and the battleground ... The stakes in this battle are not the territory, commercial advantages, or political leverage of ordinary wars, but the mind and destiny of man.*[4]

Indeed, the mind, soul, and destiny of man are at stake.

THE MEN IN BLACK — MIND GAMES

The MIB (Men In Black) concept is known to all UFO researchers. There are numerous UFO contactees who tell of being visited by mysterious men whom they first take to be from the CIA, KGB, NSA, FBI, or other intelligence service. These men warn the contactee to remain silent about his experience. If physical evidence of a CE-2 is in the possession of the contactee, they try to take possession of it. Often they harass the individual. Many victims later claim that they realize that the MIB are actually aliens themselves.

At first glance this is one of the strangest aspects of our studies of UFOs. Why would UFO beings contact mankind, only to later attempt to hide all evidence of their appearance and to threaten the contactee not to reveal what he had experienced?

The MIB visit is not an uncommon experience of UFO contactees. The MIBs often pose as government agents. They are described as wearing black hats, black trench coats, and dark glasses. They demand that the contactee give up any physical evidence that was left behind by the UFO. They threaten the contactee with dire consequences if he dares to reveal what he knows. Inevitably, the contactee gets the idea that these are not normal people. Usually the disguise is less than perfect: the eyes can be seen as alien eyes; the hands are not like human hands; or there is just "something about them" that makes the contactee realize that they were "aliens." In some cases the MIB steal or coverup the evidence of the UFO landing and ETI contact. Sometimes they cause havoc in the life of the contactee.

What possible purpose would this serve? First, this makes the UFO experience more credible. After all, according to the UFO advocates, if the ETIs are making their first tentative contacts, they may want to disguise the fact until the "right time." The contactee believes that they are seeking to keep their visits secret. In some cases the contactee is told this upon subsequent visitations. This serves to convince him that "aliens" really have visited him, not only initially, but on later encounters.

Secondly, this is a diversionary tactic. The MIB so confuse the contactee that he cannot really evaluate what is happening to him. He is worried about further problems he might encounter. He is terrified into silence. Only after further contact and "enlightenment" is he allowed to talk freely about his experience. This smoke-screen serves the demonic powers behind the experience. They use fear and confusion to weaken a person until they have complete control. When they can "trust" the contactee, he will do what they want. This kind of experience is not unique to UFO encounters. This has been known among occult devotees for centuries. Brad Steiger writes of the parallel between the MIB and the occult experience:

> *The Brothers of the Shadow, like the MIB, are known for threatening students of the occult whenever they get too close to lifting the Veil of Isis. As Madame Blavatsky says when referring to the Brothers of the Shadow, they are "the leading stars" on the great spiritual stage of "materialization."* [5]

The "Veil of Isis" is an occultic term describing when the devotee encounters the goddess and uncovers her nature. Then the devotee can enter the deepest mysteries of occult practices. Could this describe the condition of a person who is possessed? The threat causes one to want that which is forbidden even more. The devotee has already tasted forbidden fruit. Any further prohibition simply strengthens his desire for more.

Another possible effect of the MIB visits may be that the UFO contactee is only driven to further encounters with these deceivers to sort out his confusion or to assure himself that they really do mean him no harm or that he really has seen something and is not merely insane. Perhaps it is also a captor-captive syndrome. This causes the contactee to sympathize and even cooperate more fully with his captors to make their displeasure less severe. In each experience he loses more of his will to that of the alien.

The MIB and the Brothers of the Shadow can be viewed as the same demonic beings. Confusion and terror is useful to the enemy in controlling and conditioning anyone being overtaken. Brad Steiger writes of one victim of the MIB experience: "At times she seemed almost to be possessed."[6] This is the purpose of MIB: to bring a person into subjection and control. By using the initial hallucinatory experience of UFO contact and subsequently the MIB threat, the contactee is subjected to a mind-control, brainwashing technique designed to break down his will and resistance to eventual possession.

BARNEY AND BETTY HILL — KIDNAPED BY A UFO

One of the best documented cases of UFO abduction happened on September 19-20 in 1961. Here is the story of Barney and Betty Hill. The Hills were returning from a short vacation trip near the Canadian border to their home in Portsmouth, New Hampshire. When they were in the vicinity of the White Mountains, they experienced a strange event that plagued both of their lives for many years to come. There were two to three hours of missing time in their return trip for which neither of them could account. Both had vague fears, bad dreams, and a suspicion that something strange and horrible had happened to them. To sort out their experience, they entered long term psychoanalysis. During their sessions with Dr. Benjamin Simon, both revealed events that they had suppressed for two years. Even after six months of initial treatment in 1963 and 1964 and later follow-up sessions in 1966, they still had some very disturbing dreams and ongoing fear about what happened to them.

During hypnotic regression the Hills remembered that they sighted an object that at first was thought to be a satellite or an airplane. As the object drew nearer and seemed to follow them, they began to be both afraid and fascinated. Their dog cowered and whined on the seat beside them. They felt they were being "observed." Betty looked at the object through a set of binoculars that they had with them. She saw a disk with lights on the edge. She asked Barney to look at it. Eventually, Barney stopped their car and got out to look at the object through his binoculars. In spite of some apprehension, he walked toward the object hovering a couple hundred feet away. He felt drawn toward it. He came running back terrified and crying in near hysteria. They began to drive off in an attempt to "get away" until they heard a beeping in the trunk of their car. When they heard this beeping, they became very drowsy. Later, after hearing the beeps for a second time, they began to regain their full consciousness. They were some distance from the initial encounter with the object and the place where they heard the first set of beeps. Upon arriving home both felt strange and clammy. They felt dirty. Something very unsettling had happened to them.

Barney relates his confusion and fear after arriving home,

Betty said she wanted me to throw the food from the refrigerator (in their car) out, and to keep the rest of the things from the car out of the house. I could hardly wait until I was able to get everything from the car to the back porch so that I could go into the bathroom, where I took a mirror and began looking over my body. And I don't know, I didn't know why at the time, but I felt unclean with a grime different from what usually accumulates on a trip. Somewhat clammy, Betty and I both went to the window, and then opened the back door, and we both looked skyward. And I went into the bathroom and looked around. I can't describe it — it was a presence. Not that the presence was there with us, but something very puzzling had happened. [7]

Betty also felt contaminated by the experience:

Up to that point, Betty's floating anxiety about some kind of contamination had been instinctive; now she wondered if there were some kind of basis in reality for the feelings she had. [8]

Subsequently, they had dreams and fears that caused them to look for an answer to what they had experienced. They reported the incident, talked to UFO experts, and eventually sought therapy for their anxieties and fears. While it is not the purpose of this book to discuss psycho-analysis or the conclusions at which they eventually arrived through hypnosis therapy, we must note that both Freudian and Jungian psycho-analysis have occultic associations. We would also have grave reservations about hypnosis because it has occultic connections. But the results of their sessions do give us some evidence of the experience they had in the White Mountains. This will point us toward a disturbing conclusion. The Hills had an encounter with evil, spiritual beings who led them to believe they had encountered a UFO and ETIs.

Barney related the ability of the UFO beings to command his obedience. Even though Barney wanted to run or resist, he couldn't. The following quotes from his therapy will illustrate this:

> And he's looking at me. And just telling me: "Don't be afraid ... Stay there — and just keep looking. Just keep looking — and stay there..."[9]

> "Yes. Just stay there," he said. (Now his voice breaks in extreme terror.) It's pounding in my head! (He screams again.) I gotta get away! I gotta get away from here! ... His eyes! His eyes. I've never seen eyes like that before.[10]

> I don't know. I've never seen eyes slanted like that.[11]

> Oh, those eyes! They're in my brain![12]

> Oh — oh, the eyes are there. Always the eyes are there. And they're telling me I don't have to be afraid.[13]

> Yes. They won't talk to me. Only the eyes are talking to me. I — I — I — I don't understand that. Oh — the eyes don't have a body. They're just eyes.[14]

> All I see are these eyes ... I'm not even afraid that

they're not connected to a body. They're just here. They're just up close to me, pressing against my eyes. That's funny. I'm not afraid.[15]

And the eyes. The eyes seemed to be coming toward me. Then I heard myself saying that the eyes seemed to be burning into my senses, like an indelible imprint.[16]

The power of hypnotic control over Barney was such that he no longer was able to resist the experience. He had a sense of being "suspended" or out of touch and control over his body. This is a common sensation of a person under a deep hypnotic trance state.

No. I'm just suspended. I'm just floating about.[17]

And they began coming toward me ... And they came and assisted me ... I felt very weak, but I wasn't afraid ... I feel like I am dreaming ... I am there — and I am not there.[18]

Let us evaluate the images that the therapist recalled from Barney's experience. First there was a very strange aspect to the experience. He saw beings, but the beings seemed to be revealed on more than one level. He saw an appearance of bodies, a spacecraft, and all the accompanying aspects of UFO encounters. These are on one level. On the other level were eyes that were not connected to bodies at all. These eyes were able to control Barney Hill and even penetrate his mind. We believe that the appearance of a UFO craft and crew members could have been hallucinatory or illusionary. Perhaps they were an induced experience to make Barney Hill think he was encountering a UFO and ETIs. The penetrating eyes were the real experience. These were the eyes of a spiritual entity. The induced vision of UFOs and ETIs could not cover the evil of the entity's hypnotic powers.

Second, the longer Barney looked at them, the less frightened he grew. These evil eyes were able to hypnotize and control Barney Hill. His will to resist was completely overruled by the power of the eyes. Occult literature abounds with references to the "evil eye." The deceivers use their ability to capture the attention and subsequently the will of those they are seeking to influence. Betty Hill also reveals the fear that she felt on that night. Like Barney, the longer that the event continued, the more she seemed to be under its control. She says,

I think it was the same one I was watching in the sky. And there were trees and a path, and there was this clearing. And they're taking me up to the object. I don't want to go on it ... I don't know what's going to happen if I do. I don't want to go ... So he, and one of the others, each take my arm, and I get sort of a helpless feeling. There's not much I can do at this point, but to go on with them...[19]

After entering the "object," Betty was forced to undergo a physical examination.

I'm on the table and the leader, they had hurt me by putting a needle in my navel. And the leader had run his hand in front of my eyes ... I didn't have any more pain.[20]

Because, it was such, so much pain...[21]

Barney was also forced to undergo a "medical" procedure that he did not want to experience.

But I'm afraid to open my eyes, because I am being told strongly by myself to keep my eyes closed, and don't open them. And I don't want to be operated on.[22]

During her encounter, Betty thought the "aliens" had done a very painful test on her. When the leader of the "aliens" passed his hand over her eyes, the pain ceased. Barney felt he was operated upon against his will. Consider for one moment what is being revealed. These beings inflicted pain in a forced experience. Neither Barney nor Betty were willing participants. That in itself is not benevolent. Forced experiences such as this and those that are even more horrible in other cases are more in keeping with an evil intention toward humans.

The "aliens" were also able to cause the pain to cease by an act that resembles the power that a hypnotist uses on his subjects. Could it not be that the reason they could do this is that the whole experience, pain included, was induced by demonically controlled hypnotic suggestion?

Barney and Betty continued to reveal the non-physical, hallucinatory aspect of the experience in the way in which the beings communicated. It was not with vocalized words, but with a telepathic power. Barney said,

He did not speak by word. I was told what to do by his thoughts making my thoughts understand.[23]

I could understand his thoughts. His thoughts came to me like your thoughts — when you (the hypnotist/therapist) talk to me...[24]

The "aliens" used telepathic powers to communicate. A significant thing is that Barney felt that the communication with the "aliens" was going on in the context of a hypnotic trance like the one the therapist used. Barney sensed that he was in a trance-like state during the event.

Betty also felt that the communication was not vocal, but telepathic.

Betty said that somehow now she cannot believe she communicated with these creatures ... by word of mouth.[25]

I did not hear an actual voice. But in my mind, I knew what he was saying ... It was more as if the words were there, a part of me, and he was outside the actual creation of the words themselves.[26]

Telepathic communication is not a normal characteristic of beings in our own level of existence. It is more in keeping with spiritual entities. Both of the Hills had years of fear and nightmares as a result of their episode in the White Mountains. Over five years later Barney still relived the horror of that night. He still grew nearly hysterical at the memory of it.

> *I-I didn't like them putting their hands on me! (His breathing becomes fast and excited.) ... (Begins to sob heavily.) I didn't like them putting their hands on me! I don't like them touching me!* [27]

Betty realized that both she and Barney would never be the same after the encounter. Barney had continuing nightmares and she had a persisting fear.

> *Barney's been having nightmares all week.* [28]

> *If I could get over being afraid. Right now I think I'd die of fright if I saw them again.* [29]

I sympathize with the Hills. No human should be made to encounter such things. However, more and more people are encountering the spiritual realm. What they are finding there is not always good. Those who do not believe in the Lord Jesus Christ as their personal Saviour have no protection from the deceptive powers of Satan's realm.

Barney and Betty Hill saw something on that September night. Perhaps it was not a spacecraft but a demonically created illusion and an induced experience. Their wills were overpowered, and they were deceived in an attempt to create an incident that would give credibility to the UFO lie. The real nature of the encounter was that of two humans confronting an evil and deceptive power. Others have had similar stories to tell. Later cases reveal even more vividly the evil mind behind the UFO experience.

The Hills experienced something similar to an MIB effect subsequent to their encounter. This is the reason they could not remember much of the experience until undergoing therapy. This tactic of the enemy gives an added "credibility" to their experience. The fact that they were "told" to forget by the "aliens," only later to remember the event, gives an appearance of reality and mystery that promotes the UFO deception.

Finally, we do not know whether everything that they revealed in therapy happened to them. It could have been a deceptive illusion. In any event, the Hills encountered something terrible and evil in the White Mountains. We probably will never know all the reasons why the Hills were beset by these evil, spiritual beings in 1961. It is enough that they were. The tragic postscript to the Hills' misadventures with the UFOs was that Barney died a premature death. Betty Hill is convinced that her husband died as an aftereffect of the physical examination he underwent on the alien craft. Was it merely a hypnotically induced illusion? Was the craft an actual materialization? These are questions that we cannot answer at the present time. We do know that many people are undergoing bad experiences in this realm.

UFO and ETI advocates use the Hills' encounter to prove their theory. However, a closer look at such experiences reveals something very distressing. The deceivers are stepping up their activity in our generation.

On the positive side, for Bible-believing Christians, we can expect two things. First, the Lord will grant us more strength to overcome these deceptive tactics of the enemy. We can confidently expose and resist the deception Satan is using to control people. Second, the Lord is coming back to Earth. Events going on in the world at this time cause us to look up in victory — Jesus is coming!

THE EXPERIENCE OF WHITLEY STRIEBER

Whitley Streiber was involved in a more recent abduction case in upstate New York. His experience is described in two books, *Communion* and *Transformation*. Streiber admits previous occult interest and involvement.

Streiber's experience is much more horrible in the depth of the overt evil that the "aliens" exhibited toward him. This provides us an even greater understanding of the nature of the beings that UFO abductees are encountering.

Because the deceivers are growing bolder, we can see more clearly the satanic power behind the UFO event. Texe Marrs describes Streiber's initial encounter and makes some startling observations:

> *Three fascinating yet horrifying things happened to Whitley Strieber that awful night in his isolated home in upstate New York. First he claims that while held captive by the aliens, he underwent what can only be interpreted as a sexual initiation by an alluring yet despicable-looking female alien. Strieber evidently believes this being may have been Ishtar, the Mother Goddess of ancient Babylon ... Second, Strieber recalls that as he struggled, cried and screamed to his captors, "You have no right to do this to me. I am a human being," he was confronted with a firm rebuttal from this "Mother Goddess" who was the leader of the other UFO aliens. Staring at him with eyes that reached to the very core of his being, she sternly replied, "We do have a right!" ... Third, we read in* Communion *that Strieber subsequently woke up to discover etched on his arm a mark.* [31]

Forceful rape and a luciferic initiation do not sound benevolent. Remember that most people who are UFO advocates believe that the aliens are basically interested in our welfare and spiritual evolution. This experience reveals that they are interested in control through possession! Concerning Streiber's forceful rape, we believe this could have been a mentally induced experience, not a physical rape. However, there could very well be physical evidence in such cases. Demons can manipulate a person's mind. They can also manipulate physical reality. Streiber protested his abduction and rape. Did the demonic powers behind it have a right to do these things to him because Streiber had indulged in occultic practices?

The UFO aliens in this case are linked to Ishtar! This is enlightening, since this is the same demonic entity that pagans worshiped as Astarte or Diana. The real identity of these ETIs becomes obvious to anyone who reads the Bible — they are evil. We do not believe the claim of demons is valid or unbreakable. A person who has had this type of experience can gain total deliverance and spiritual freedom through Jesus Christ. We have no condemnation for the people who have experienced these things. They are simply victims who have been misused by the deceivers. Rather than condemn these unfortunate people, we hold out the hope of the gospel as a means to personal salvation and freedom from all demonic bondage!

We are not prepared to state that any of the people mentioned in this book are possessed. That is between them and God. Only if a person comes to us for counsel could we make such an evaluation. Of course the deceivers work for full possession of each victim, not only the UFO contactee, but in many other ways and realms. Texe Marrs' description of the progression from initial fear to luciferic initiation is found in his book, *Mystery Mark of the New Age,* and the progression from an initial fear to ultimate acceptance of the demonic experience is revealed in Marrs' observation concerning luciferic initiation:

> *These feelings, voiced by so many who have received a luciferic Initiation, are significant. They point to two inescapable facts: (1) The initiate recognizes beforehand that he is coming into close contact with dark, evil forces, and a spirit of fear engulfs him; and (2) after the initiation is over and Satan's demons have taken residence inside the individual, his mind is patently altered. This is what New Agers call the Kundalini or Skaktipat experience, technically termed a paradigm (world-view) shift.* [32]

Many well-known contactees have experienced this initial fear and revulsion at their contact with the UFO beings. As their experience progressed, they eventually resigned themselves to it. They were victimized. It is interesting that a paradigm shift takes place in the abductee. This is the same world-view shift that many New Agers advocate. After contact the abductee usually is convinced of the reality of UFOs and ETIs. In addition, some contactees become convinced that they are chosen to preach the "aliens" New Age gospel to others.

In Streiber's case we see the methods that aliens used to break down his resistance. The book *Transformation,* the sequel to *Communion,* reveals ominous aspects of his experience. It sounds like demonic harassment. The entities seemed to be toying with his mind. He experienced both "good" and "bad alien" entities. The "bad aliens" terrified him. The "good aliens" came, soothed his fears, and comforted him. The "good" were then readily accepted because of the experiences that the "bad" caused him to have in the first place. The fact is that the "good aliens" and "bad aliens" are the same.

This kind of brainwashing and will-destroying technique is used on POW's in countries that do not abide by the Geneva Conventions. Torture and fear are inflicted, then relief is promised if the person cooperates. Police sometimes use a technique called "good cop — bad cop." One policeman is angry, mean, and aggressive. The good cop uses gentle sympathy and persuasion. The purpose is to make the suspect want to cooperate with the friendly cop. This is an illustration of what Streiber experienced and described in his book, *Transformation.*

In one experience, he realized or sensed that the entities were about to make contact with him. He grew tired and resigned himself to it. This indicates a large measure of control over his will.

> *There was no question of my doing anything about the fact that I knew the visitors were here. It was all I could do to climb the stairs to the bedroom.*[33]

He goes on to describe the menace and suffering that he felt:

> *I felt an absolutely indescribable sense of menace. It was hell on Earth to be there, and yet I could not*

*move, couldn't cry out, couldn't get away. I lay as still
as death, suffering inner agonies...* [34]

He had no strength to resist, move, cry out, or escape the
"alien" beings that came to torture him. He felt infested.

*I thought I was going to suffocate. My throat was
closed, my eyes swimming with tears. The sense of
being infested was powerful and awful...* [35]

After a night of terror, Streiber finally experienced
relief. The female being came to him to comfort him. His
will was broken. In spite of ugliness and terror he longed
for them to return!

*Again, though, I felt love. Despite all the ugliness
and the terrible things that had been done, I found
myself longing for them, missing them!* [36]

By no means do we imply that the Hills, Streiber, or
others who have had close encounters of a third or fourth
kind are evil or ill-intentioned people. All of us are born
into a flawed world. All of us are lost in sin's degradation.
God offers to each and every one a way out of the dark.
Jesus will be Saviour and Liberator to anyone who will call
on Him. Not only those who have been misused by demons
need His salvation. We all do. (See Rom. 3:23; 1 John 1:9.)
Without the protection of the Holy Spirit and the angels of
God, any of us could be subjected to demonic delusion in
these end-times.

SATAN IS ALIVE AND WELL — IN THE UFO
EXPERIENCE

We have looked at the mind-bending and will-destroying
techniques being used by the UFO deceivers. Close
encounters of the third kind usually reveal the evil intention
of the UFO astronauts. These demonic entities are waging
a war against mankind. Their tool is deception. The
battleground is the minds of men. Only in Jesus Christ, the
Son of God, is there safety. We urge each reader to find
Jesus Christ as Saviour and Lord today. The delusion is

powerful in these end-times; we cannot stand alone. Seek the fellowship of a Bible-believing church whose pastor faithfully teaches the whole Word of God.

Amazingly, a New Age author, Brad Steiger, writes about this very thing:

> *Constable warns us that the Ahrimanic (fallen angels of Persian and Chaldean tradition) emissaries appear everywhere "unrecognized and often aided by humans who don't know that the devil is alive and well — and coming to Earth within the lifetime of millions now living."* [37]

Truly, these entities are actively using deception to wage a battle for the possession of the human race. The UFO advocates are cooperating with the satanic plan by promoting the UFO delusion.

> *It is Constable's contention that humans are constantly being seduced into doing the work of the nether forces, because they simply do not know that such forces exist, let alone how they work into and upon Earth life.* [38]

Our best weapon is to be informed of the deceptive plan that is being carried out in our world today.

> *If man can be shown where the battlefield is, the nature of the terrain, and the ways in which he is already being assaulted in this inner war, then the right tactics and strategy can be brought to bear against the inimical forces.* [39]

Just what should our tactics and strategy be in this war? First of all, submission to God and resistance against the enemy is prescribed by the apostle James: "Submit yourselves therefore to God, resist the devil and he will flee from you" (James 4:7). Secondly, we must be armed with truth — the truth of God's Word! It reveals the world-view that strengthens us against all evolutionary and other schemes of deception. It shows us the promises that gird up our minds against the enemy.

For though we walk in the flesh, we do not war after the flesh: For the weapons of our warfare are not carnal, but mighty through God to the pulling down of strong holds; Casting down imaginations, and every high thing that exalteth itself against the knowledge of God, and bringing into captivity every thought to the obedience of Christ; And having in a readiness to revenge all disobedience, when your obedience is fulfilled (2 Cor. 10:3-6).

The Bible feeds our souls with the kind of truth and experience that keep us from opening ourselves to deception. Also, we must know the devices of the enemy. The UFO lie and all New Age deceptions must be revealed. Thus we not only keep ourselves from false ideas and doctrines, but we also have a ready answer to those who ask us about the hope that we possess!

But in your hearts set apart Christ as Lord. Always be prepared to give an answer to everyone who asks you to give the reason for the hope that you have (1 Pet. 3:15;NIV).

FOOTNOTES

[1]*SCP Journal,* August 1977, Vol.1 No.2, "The Modern Prometheus: Science Fiction and the New Consciousness," p.7.

[2]Brad Steiger, *The UFO Abductors,* Berkley Books, p.212.

[3]Ibid., p.213.

[4]Ibid., p.212.

[5]Brad Steiger, *Alien Meetings,* Ace Books, p.114, quoting *New Atlantean Journal,* March 1975.

[6]Ibid., p.117.

[7]John G. Fuller, *The Interrupted Journey,* Berkley Books, p.35.

[8]Ibid., p.38.

[9]Ibid., p.118.
[10]Ibid., p.119.
[11]Ibid., p.120.
[12]Ibid., p.121.
[13]Ibid., p.123.
[14]Ibid., p.124.
[15]Ibid., p.126.
[16]Ibid., p.300.
[17]Ibid., p.126.
[18]Ibid., pp.147-148.
[19]Ibid., p.191.
[20]Ibid., p.204.
[21]Ibid., p.205.
[22]Ibid., p.149.
[23]Ibid., p.240.
[24]Ibid., p.241
[25]Ibid., p.272.
[26]Ibid., p.310.
[27]Ibid., p.329
[28]Ibid., p.267.
[29]Ibid., p.268.
[30]Ibid., p.128.
[31]Texe Marrs, *Mystery Mark of the New Age,* Crossway Books, pp.36-37.
[32]Ibid., p.39.
[33]Whitley Strieber, *Transformation,* p.189.
[34]Ibid., p.190.
[35]Ibid., p.192.
[36]Ibid., p.193.
[37]Steiger, op. cit., p.213, 314.
[38]Steiger, op. cit., p.213.
[39]Steiger, op. cit., p.212. Quoting military and aviation historian Trevor James Constable.

CHAPTER TEN

WALK-INS

AVATARS, DEMONS

LAUNCHING A "BRAVE NEW WORLD"

Things have changed dramatically in the bizarre world of UFO activity in recent years. Strangest of all are things being experienced by alien contactees. As Alice in Wonderland said, "Curiouser and curiouser!" A few years ago, UFOs were dismissed as the lunatic fringe. Now they are being thoughtfully considered. Data is carefully analyzed by scientists, military leaders, and politicians. Go to the public library and take a look at all the UFO books. Note the quality of some of the writers. Magazine and newspaper articles, television "documentary" dramas, such as the one recently seen on CBS, portray UFOs as a reality to be reckoned with.

People are no longer satisfied with just reading about UFOs. Many seek to see one. Some seek contact by various means. The deceivers are more than willing to accommodate them!

A New Age devotee just hasn't "arrived" unless he has had contact with a "spirit guide," an "ascended master," a "channeled entity," or a "space brother-ETI." Contact is sought through meditation techniques, invocation, luciferic initiation, or by the laying-on-of-hands by a guru, channelor, or other New Age expert.

SATANIC MIND-PROGRAMMING

A few years ago the frightening prospect of the UFO experience's being a part of a larger satanic plan was proposed as a very real possibility. It was predicted others would come along who would complete the full circle of delusion with a theory that would reinterpret the very nature and person of God. The ancient astronaut theory of von Daniken and colleagues presents just such an idea, as first expressed in *Chariots of the Gods*. Dr. Clifford Wilson, a brilliant Christian archaeologist and researcher proposed the following idea:

> *Hypnotism and temporary paralysis are commonly associated with UFOs. Are men being programmed? If people are being hypnotized, is it possible that some are being "programmed" for something too horrible to contemplate? ... If the devil knows his time is short, he might well be programming men — and others — to obey when a signal is given, a signal that they will be programmed to obey but are not now aware of.*[1]

It is no longer merely a possibility. The experiences of many people point to the connection between the UFO experience, the New Age, and the end-time deception. One New Age writer, Brad Steiger, describes how he came to write one of his books:

> *The inspiration for the book came after a visitation from a spiritual being that materialized before me on two consecutive nights. Although I crumpled into unconsciousness at the outset of each encounter and consciously remembered hearing only an initial word or two from the entity, I awakened on the dawn after the second visit with the ideas for* The Divine Fire *bubbling in my brain...*[2]

Steiger's book is filled with the experiences of trance mediums, channelors, New Age adepts, occult practitioners, UFO contactees, and Spirit-filled Christians. All these experiences are mixed together as various aspects of the

same experience! It is wrong to equate the actions and work of the Spirit of God with the experiences of trance mediums. There is absolutely no connection between the two. (See Mark 3:28,29.)
Steiger clearly perceives the relationship between UFO/ETI experiences and the metaphysical or occult realm. What he does not distinguish is the demonic deception behind these phenomena. The devil is programming minds today. Through various encounters Satan is transforming civilization's ideas about reality. He is preparing for the coming shift in perception that is necessary to condition people to accept the Antichrist, who could be alive in the world today.

COME RIGHT IN — INVASION OF THE BODY SNATCHERS

Ruth Montgomery, a New Age author, is a trance medium. Most of the content of her books is dictated by her "spirit guides." She writes extensively about the experiences that New Age advocates are having with "spirit entities." Her teaching is in line with that of Steiger and other UFO spokespersons. One type of spirit she talks a lot about are the walk-ins. According to her there are higher spirits, ascended masters who are now on Earth seeking embodiment inside of living humans. Of the walk-in spirits Montgomery says:

A walk-in is a high-minded entity who is permitted to take over the body of another human being who wishes to depart.[3]

The walk-ins, so-called, are superior but not perfected souls who have gone on after many earthly lives...[4]

Ruth Montgomery makes three assumptions. First, she assumes that the beings have a benevolent nature. We believe that they are the deceivers who seek to destroy us. Second, she assumes that the spirits are beings who have gone through a process of evolution to a higher spiritual plane. Third, she assumes that the doctrine of reincarnation is valid. It is interesting to note that reincarnation for Western mankind is not the same as taught in the East. Eastern reincarnation sees the possibility of a person's coming back as an animal or a tree. It is more palatable for Western people to think only of coming back in human form, unless the even more desirable higher spiritual level can be attained.

Of course, people do not come back at all! We cannot achieve perfection through repeated cycles of existence. The only answer to sin is to accept the ransom Jesus paid for us when He died in our place on the cross of Golgotha. Life is not a nine inning baseball game. The Bible clearly teaches that we receive only one inning in this world. If we strike out in the first inning, we do not get another chance at bat!

For it is appointed unto man ONCE to die, and after this the judgment (Heb. 9:27).

If the walk-ins are not evolved, ascended beings, who are they? They are demons disguised as "not perfected souls." Their purpose is to possess individuals and to prepare the human race for the paradigm shift and the revelation of the Antichrist. Alert, informed Christians have nothing to fear.

Montgomery is told by her "spirit-guides" that walk-ins have the welfare of the persons they infest in mind. The "spirit guides" ask,

What is so strange, they ask, about a walk-in with good motivation taking over a body, when the world is aware that evil entities can "possess" occupied bodies and cause untold suffering? [5]

Isn't it odd that some New Age advocates claim the ability to distinguish between benevolent and evil entities? If these beings are more intelligent than humans, wouldn't they have the ability to conceal their true intentions? The

New Age advocates think they can out-smart spiritual entities that are capable of incredible deception. However, many are being possessed by evil spirits, deluded into thinking they are benevolent beings who will enhance human consciousness and lift the person into self-realization and Godhood.

The source of these experiences is revealed by the teaching of the entities. Dr. I.D.E. Thomas observes the following:

> *Many of their messages contradict the gospel of Jesus Christ. They advocate such propositions as*
>
> * *An impersonal God;*
> * *Reincarnation and endless improvement in the hereafter;*
> * *Men are not lost sinners in need of divine mercy;*
> * *Christ was divine only in the sense that all men are divine; and*
> * *Christ's resurrection was a mere materialization.*
>
> *These revelations clearly indicate a suspicious source.*[6]

These ideas are occultic, New Age doctrines. They are inspired by demons. The apostle Paul wrote,

> *Now the Spirit speaketh expressly, that in the latter times some shall depart from the faith, giving heed to seducing spirits, and doctrines of devils ...* (1 Tim. 4:1).

In the UFO realm there is no absolute truth. There is no stable measure of what is true or false. There are many New Age "bibles" but they all say "Your reality is not necessarily my reality. Each one of us creates his own reality." This produces an absolute anarchy in which each person becomes a law unto himself or herself. Everyone can decide whether the alien experience is real or not. This chaos is not of God, for as the Bible says, "God is not the author of confusion."

Believers in Jesus Christ have the one answer that is not subjective, changing, and uncertain. It is revealed in the Bible, which is true, unchanging, and certain!

> We have also a more sure word of prophecy; whereunto ye do well that ye take heed, as unto a light that shineth in a dark place, until the day dawn, and the day star arise in your hearts: Knowing this first, that no prophecy of the scripture is of any private interpretation. For the prophecy came not in old time by the will of man: but holy men of God spake as they were moved by the Holy Ghost (2 Pet. 1:19-21).

UFOs AND ETIs

Ruth Montgomery writes about UFOs and ETIs in her book, *Strangers Among Us*. The "guides" explain the nature of the ETIs to her:

> Suffice it to say that the UFOs are from outer space, and that the souls who operate and often inhabit them are sentient beings who are in a totally different stage of advancement than are Earthlings.[7]

The deceptive spirits that she trusts so implicitly tell her that these UFO operators are evolved space beings. Curiously, they are said to be "souls." (Remember that "walk-ins" are also said to be "not perfected souls.") A measure of truth may be disclosed here. The UFOs and ETIs are not physical at all. They are spiritual entities. They are a spiritual manifestation. This idea slips out again in another place. A man possessed by an "alien" talks about a photograph of a UFO:

> ...the photograph was really an illusion; that it was not a photograph of physical matter, and humans were wrong in perceiving it as physical matter.[8]

These spirits are coming with increasing regularity. Our period of history has seen and will see even more frequent manifestations of such things. The Bible refers to increasing demonic activity in the end-times. (See Rev. 9:1-11.)

Montgomery relates that they are coming in increasing numbers because they are interested in the events that are an indication of the emerging New Age. But the fact is that these demonic entities are attempting to lead man into a New Age characterized by a world-wide rebellion against God and His purposes.

For they are the spirits of devils, working miracles, which go forth unto the kings of the earth and of the whole world, to gather them to the battle of that great day of God Almighty (Rev. 16:14).

THE NIGHT SHIFT —
DARKNESS COVERS THE EARTH

Montgomery writes of a coming shift in the Earth's axis, a catastrophic time of cleansing, and an emergence of a new humanity. The increasing numbers of UFOs, ETIs, and walk-ins are related to this coming shift. Her "spirit guides" tell her,

But the extraterrestrials are coming in increasing numbers... [9]

The extraterrestrials are indeed fascinated by the coming shift... [10]

Why are they increasing in numbers at this time? She tells us:

...I write a book to help prepare readers for the coming shift of the earth on its axis, which they say will occur near the close of this century, after a devastating war. [11]

There will be terrible wars in the last days. Right now we are engaged in intense spiritual warfare. The ultimate battle is not nation against nation. It is a war between spiritual forces. Human beings have a choice of sides. We can choose Christ or Antichrist. We can choose God or

Satan. The deceivers will do everything in their power to lead us away from the Almighty. God will not force us to follow Him. He allows us to make up our mind. If that were not true, then we would be mere automatons or slaves. Some people will not be fooled by the UFO hoax but will be nevertheless deceived in another way. The enemy is clever and has many ways of reaching people for his destructive purposes. The increasing numbers of UFOs, ETIs, walk-ins, and spirit guides are the spear-heading attack forces of Satan's end-time assault on humanity and upon the Creator himself. The coming events will be a time of great trouble in the earth. Mankind is under assault. Demonic powers take advantage of present day confusion, causing people to seek answers to our overwhelming global problems. They promise help from "higher beings." Their purpose is to prepare humanity for the short reign of the Antichrist.

If our calculations are right there will be a massive open manifestation of alien presence and power on Earth. Something big is about to happen! Kings, prime ministers, and presidents will tremble before the "ascended masters." How could they refuse the help so generously offered when Earth is about to self-destruct? They will play right into the hands of the Antichrist if they follow the aliens' suggestions. Some rulers may be executed by angry mobs for taking a stand against the "space brothers."

An axis-shift and concurrent disasters are related to the "paradigm shift" that New Age devotees expect in the near future. This shift in humanity's world-view will be precipitated by massive demonic deception and even possession.

What mankind needs, however, is not a New Age paradigm shift but a good dose of truth and reality. Man needs the truth of the gospel of Jesus Christ and the reality of sins forgiven and eternal life!

VARIETIES OF ALIEN MANIFESTATIONS — DIFFERENT BUT THE SAME

What at first appears to be a wide variety of different strange encounters, is a many-faceted, unified plan of deception. UFOs, ETIs, walk-ins, occult meditation, channeling, New Age, higher self, et al., are the work of the same deceivers. They all make the same final declaration. New Ager Ruth Montgomery comes to the following conclusion:

To the limit of my understanding, it would seem that the Guides have identified three types of beings who have achieved sufficient advancement to enter our earth plane, and appear in solid form to us...

Apparently the highest achievers in this category are the avatars, who can come and go at will, and who, according to the Guides, are in touch with outer-space beings as well as with humans on Planet Earth. The second type is the Walk-ins, who have always been Earthlings but are high-minded, advanced souls who return to adult bodies in order to accelerate the progress of their fellow-men. The third class is the extraterrestrials, who, still few, have allegedly found the means of penetrating the earth's atmosphere and occupying bodies of adult humans, for limited scientific experiments and observations of our planetary changes.[12]

The overlooked reality behind these observations is that they are all the same entities. Steiger concludes that this might be the case:

I cannot help questioning whether the Space brothers might not be angels, spirit guides, and other messengers hiding themselves in more contemporary, and thereby more acceptable, personae.[13]

These beings are hiding themselves, lying to man. They are evil beings who hate mankind with unabated fury.

Having followed Lucifer in the earliest rebellion against God, they cannot stand the thought that redeemed humans might take their place in eternity. Those who follow the deceivers, those who allow them to "walk in" and take possession, become pawns in the final conflict, the war for control of humanity and planet Earth. The fact that these "avatars," "aliens," and "walk-ins" are all the same entities is also revealed in a discussion that Montgomery had with her "guides":

> *I asked about the different means used by space beings to enter our culture, and the Guides said that some are being born into human bodies for the first time, some have lived here upon occasion before, some are arriving as Walk-ins, and others are temporarily exchanging bodies with Earthlings "with or without permission."* [14]

It is ominous to consider that some people on Earth are inhabited by the alien entities "with or without permission." The experience of Whitley Streiber, which we describe in another chapter, illustrates this. He tried to resist but was told that the "alien" had the right to enter without his permission.

Many people naively seek to contact "aliens," "spirit guides," or the "ascended masters." Brad Steiger's sympathy seems to be on the side of the aliens. He says,

> *By mutual agreement between a planetary dweller and an inhabitant of our craft, the knowledge and the memory of one of us may be blended with the planetary inhabitant without the loss of the receiver's identity.* [15]

In spite of his enthusiasm about this experience and his encouragement for others to seek it, Steiger has some reservations:

> *I had the uneasy feeling that the ecstatic flame may, in reality, have been kindled by multidimensional beings who have a kind of symbiotic relationship with*

*man and who may exploit their "prophets" for selfish,
parasitical purposes.*[16]

One of the people that Steiger interviewed was a man
named Charles. He was deeply involved in the New Age as
a trance medium for an entity named Ishkomar. In the
trance channeling sessions that Steiger recorded in his
book, this entity spoke horrible blasphemies against God,
Jesus, and the Bible. The things he taught were the same
occultic ideas that have been taught by adepts through the
centuries.

The initial contact Charles had with the beings, who
later took control of his life, seemed so innocent. Steiger
relates the invitation that Charles gave during the contact:

*"I'm just a little guy," Charles had said, speaking
to the UFO. "But I'm friendly. I would like to be your
friend."*[17]

So many people are like Charles. They begin by looking
for a friendly contact with some "alien" being. If the "alien"
finds a receptivity, the contact proceeds until the person is
possessed by the powers behind the UFO/ETI.

Charles intended only to have the friendship of the
aliens. What he received was the absolute domination of
his being.

Steiger relates an incident experienced by his wife and
himself. He heard a buzzing sound enter the bedroom, saw
a green orb of light, and observed this thing enter his wife's
open mouth one night. Immediately after seeing this he
also slipped into unconsciousness. He tells of the similarity
of this experience to that of channelors, UFOs, and
poltergeists:

*A number of revelators and UFO contactees have
since mentioned to me that just before the appearance
of an entity they were aware of a strange buzzing
sound. Witnesses of unexplained aerial phenomenon
have also referred to a buzzing or rushing sound
shortly before the "flying saucer" appeared over them.*

> *I am also reminded that a great deal of poltergeist activity produces a preparatory "signal" of a buzzing, rasping, or winding noise.*[18]

Steiger evidently has no fear of what happened to his wife and himself.

In his book *Mystery Mark of the New Age*, Marrs wrote this:

> *These feelings, voiced by so many who have received a Luciferic Initiation, are significant. They point to two inescapable facts: (1) The initiate recognizes beforehand that he is coming into close contact with dark, evil forces, and a spirit of fear engulfs him; and (2) after the initiation is over and Satan's demons have taken residence inside the individual, his mind is patently altered. This is what New Agers call the Kundalini or Skaktipat experience, technically termed a Paradigm (World-view) Shift.*[19]

The initial fear of possession is replaced by acceptance. This is because the mind of the person is changed, programmed to accept the deception. Marrs writes,

> *Whitley Strieber, author of* Communion, *was visited by the Babylonian goddess Ishtar in images given him by demonic entities. Not only did he have sexual relations with her, but, Strieber claimed, Ishtar and her companions were able to touch his head with a magic wand of some kind so that images began to swirl about in his mind. In effect, Strieber's mind was being programmed by these images.*[20]

This is the paradigm shift that "walk-ins," "ETIs," and "higher beings" of New Age experiences are creating. Texe Marrs comments:

> *Why was Whitley Strieber chosen to be victimized by Satan and fed these images that so totally engrossed and warped his mind? The answer is simple: Strieber himself chose to serve the devil. He did so by rejecting*

Jesus Christ, and then dabbling in the occult.[21]

What these entities are teaching is described in the Bible as when men will "believe the lie" of the Antichrist.

The coming of the lawless one will be in accordance with the work of Satan displayed in all kinds of counterfeit miracles, signs and wonders, and in every sort of evil that deceives those who are perishing. They perish because they refused to love the truth and so be saved. For this reason God sends them a powerful delusion so that they will believe the lie and so that all will be condemned who have not believed the truth but have delighted in wickedness (2 Thess. 2:9-12).

Those who become entangled in this web of deception and potential possession have one hope — Jesus can set them free!

Who hath delivered us from the power of darkness, and hath translated us into the kingdom of his dear Son: In whom we have redemption through his blood, even the forgiveness of sins (Col. 1:13,14)

FOOTNOTES

[1]Clifford Wilson, PH.D., *Gods in Chariots and Other Fantasies,* Creation Life Publishers, p.85.

[2]Brad Steiger, *Revelation: The Divine Fire,* A Berkley Book, p.vii.

[3]Ruth Montgomery, *Strangers Among Us* (This book was written through RM by demonic entities she calls her "guides."), Fawcett/Crest, p.11.

[4]Ruth Montgomery, *Herald of the New Age,* Fawcett/Crest, p.192.

[5]Ibid., p.199.

[6]Dr. I.D.E. Thomas, "Flying Saucers: Is There Something Demonic About UFO 'Messages'?" *Dove Christian Magazine,* Vol.I, No.1, 1987, p.25.

[7]Ruth Montgomery, *Strangers Among Us,* Fawcett/Crest, p.138.

[8]Ibid., p.144.

[9]Ibid., p.143.

[10]Ibid., p.143.

[11]Ibid., p.15.

[12]Ruth Montgomery, *Strangers Among Us,* Fawcett/Crest, pp.147-148.

[13]Brad Steiger, *Revelation: The Divine Fire,* A Berkley Book, p.148.

[14]Ruth Montgomery, *Aliens Among Us,* Fawcett/Crest, p.13.

[15]Brad Steiger, *Revelation: The Divine Fire,* A Berkley Book, p.141.

[16]Ibid., p.8.

[17]Ibid., p.143.

[18]Ibid., p.92.

[19]Texe Marrs, *Mystery Mark of the New Age,* Crossway Books, p.39.

[20]Ibid., p.141.

[21]Ibid., p.143.

CHAPTER ELEVEN

UFOs IN THE AGE OF AQUARIUS

NEW AGE OUTER SPACE CONNECTION

The connection between UFOs and the occult is an important facet of the UFO puzzle. Noting that all (as far as we know) recorded cases of CE-3 contacts with the "aliens" have happened to people already involved in metaphysics, crystal healing, astrology, witchcraft, spirit channeling, and so on, strengthens our position: the UFOs are materializations or illusions accomplished by evil spirits — the deceivers. This does not refer to those who have had CE-1 or CE-2 encounters with UFOs. Millions have seen a UFO, and many have noted physical evidence of a UFO presence. By comparison only a few thousand people have had direct contact or communication with aliens.

Even if our theory is all wrong; even if we have missed the boat completely about the demonic nature of UFOs; even if all UFOs turn out to be IFOs (identifiable flying objects) such as weather balloons, mirages, or "swamp gas," this book is still significant. Why? Because the UFO idea is strong in the minds of UFO believers, and people's conduct of their lives is governed by what they believe. On the other hand, the authors do firmly believe that their idea is correct. This paragraph has been included because some are bound not to agree with us.

Now the UFO phenomenon may be playing a low key role in the end-time activities of the deceivers. At any rate we are seeing an acceleration of activity and a heightening of "faith" on the part of UFO devotees. We can anticipate some almost overwhelming events connected to visiting aliens in the near future. Seemingly obscure prophecies in the Bible are going to come into sharp focus as a result of these events.

I have been in many New Age bookstores and research centers. In each and every case I was impressed with the scope of materials available on the UFO subject. Earlier we mentioned the New Age connection. In this chapter we take a detailed look at the marriage of the New Age and the UFO, alien ascended masters idea.

Several years ago Dr. Clifford Wilson perceived the occult tie. He quotes UFO researcher and bibliographer Miss Lyn E. Catoe:

> *A large part of the available UFO literature is closely linked with mysticism and the metaphysical. It deals with subjects like mental telepathy, automatic writing, and invisible entities, as well as phenomena like poltergeist manifestations and possession ... Many of the UFO reports now being published in the popular press recount alleged incidents that are strikingly similar to demoniac possession and psychic phenomena that has long been known to theologians and para-psychologists.*[1]

Since we are trying not only to communicate our own conclusions but also to display evidence from a wide range of researchers' findings, we now call attention to the words of Randall Baer, a former New Age leader and author who became a born-again believer in Jesus Christ:

> *UFO sightings and contacts have made deep inroads into the everyday fabric of much of the New Age. More than seventy-five percent of New Agers firmly believe in the existence of hosts of alien beings*

within and around planet Earth to help in the birthing of the New Age. It is noteworthy to point out that the strong upsurge in this trend also parallels the crystal craze and the huge increases in channeling activities in the mid-to-late 80s.

With Shirley MacLaine using her powerful platform to do her part in UFO evangelism plus Whitley Strieber's national exposure through his best-selling books, Communion *and* Transformation, *the UFO issue is spreading throughout all quarters of the New Age as well as mainstream society.*[2]

Add to this the witness of Shirley MacLaine, a foremost evangelist for the New Age. Her books *Dancing In The Light, Out on a Limb,* and others have made a profound impact on millions of readers. A major television network special docu-drama exposed millions more to her New Age faith. MacLaine got her calling from Mayan, a female UFO alien who gave her the message through David, one of Shirley's gurus. MacLaine wrote,

I found people had experiences similar to mine: people involved with trance channeling, past life recall, growing spiritual awareness, and even contact with UFOs.[3]

Texe and Wanda Marrs, noted evangelical researchers of the New Age movement, relate the following:

Here is just a sample (of common New Age techniques, practices, rituals, and doctrines): Astrology, Mysticism, Sorcery, Inner healing, Crystal Powers ... Astral Travel ... Cosmic Consciousness ... Out-of-body Experiences ... Demon Speaking in Tongues ... Counterfeit Signs and Wonders ... Karma ... Spirit Channeling ... Magic / Magick ... Psychokinesis ... Sacred Sex ... Reincarnation ... Psychic Powers, UFOs...[4]

Texe Marrs places UFO religions in his guide to New

Age cults and religions:

> *Astral / Galactic ... UFO societies are often a type of Astral / Galactic cult ... But many people involved in these groups are well-educated, rational, intelligent, and thoughtful. They are not the kooks they are often made out to be by the media. Besides, careful study and examination of UFO groups reveals that there is a spiritual and religious doctrine that many of their leaders are intent on spreading to all of us.*[5]

He notes elsewhere that New Age adept J.J. Hurtag is considered an expert on UFOs. It is worth noting that Hurtag's *Keys of Enoch* promotes occultic trance states, spirit guides, visualization, higher consciousness, the ascended masters — the "brotherhood of light," the third eye — the Hindu Angi point, and mind programming of men by higher beings using the number 6-6-6!

> *The Academy for Future Science is closely connected with certain UFO groups. Hurtag, for example, is well-known among UFO authorities and considered an expert on the subject.*[6]

These are just a sample of the voluminous amount of written evidence of this sort. Any person who has read very much New Age literature cannot escape this connection. The fact that we see a connection is further proved by the things that UFO/ETI advocates reveal to us.

DAWNING OF THE AGE OF AQUARIUS — THE NEW AGE GOSPEL

Brad Steiger is a New Age advocate, trance medium, and researcher. It is enlightening to read his books about UFOs and other psychic phenomena. He has spent years interviewing contactees, trance mediums, and channeled spirits. He has summarized the UFO gospel:

> *In my Aquarian revelations I presented a distillation of the Outer Space Apocrypha that would seem to contain the basic ideas presented to the world*

by all those whom the Space Brothers selected to preach the Cosmic Gospel:

• *Man is not alone in the solar system. He has "Space Brothers" and they have come to Earth to reach him and teach him.*

• *The Space Brothers have advanced information that they wish to impart to their weaker brethren. The Space Brothers want man to join an intergalactic spiritual federation.*

• *The Space Brothers are here to teach, to help awaken man's spirit, to help man to rise to higher levels of vibration so that he may be ready to enter new dimensions...*

• *Man stands now in the transitional period before the dawn of a New Age. With peace, love, understanding, and brotherhood on man's part, he will see a great new era begin to dawn.*

• *If man should not raise his vibratory rate within a set period of time, severe Earth changes and major cataclysms will take place. Such disasters will not end the world, but shall serve as cataclysmic crucibles to burn off the dross of unreceptive humanity. Those who die in such dreadful purgings will be allowed to reincarnate on higher levels of development so that their salvation will be more readily accomplished.*[7]

In short, here is a scheme of salvation for needy man that makes an end run around Jesus Christ and cancels the necessity of the atoning work of Calvary. If UFO advocates are right, we don't need Jesus; we need the space brothers! Remember that the first "spiritual federation" was led by Lucifer, the devil. It was the earliest rebellion against the Almighty. (See Isa. 14:12-15 and Ezek. 28:12-17.) The New Testament forbids distorting the gospel or preaching another gospel (Gal. 1:6-8).

In Hinduism and other occult systems the person enters a new realm of existence by tuning his consciousness in with universal mind or soul. The "space brothers" advocate raising human consciousness through occult trance meditative states. Often an "initiation" is involved. Those who experience initiation are promised entrance to a New Age of bliss, or as Jose Arguelles puts it, "the age of flowers." New Age philosopher Barbara Marx Hubbard in her unpublished *New Age Commentary on the Book of Revelation* (we have a copy of the manuscript) calls those who will not cooperate "the bad seed." The spirit that channels through Hubbard says that the bad seed must be eliminated for the paradigm shift to take place. The paradigm shift is expected by New Agers to be complete around the year 2000. Humanity will pass from the present age of Pisces into Aquarius. Pisces means "fish." The fish symbol was commonly used by early Christians. Therefore the New Ager sees a death of the Church and the birth of a universal new religion. We could best describe the new world religion as "psychic humanism." The Antichrist who will head the New World government will be the head of this religion. Paul prophesied about the man of sin: "Who opposeth and exalteth himself above all that is called God, or that is worshipped; so that he as God sitteth in the temple of God, shewing himself that he is God" (2 Thess. 2:4).

Listen to that son of perdition (Antichrist) speaking to the inhabitants of planet Earth in the Tribulation:

> *We have proven that all old religions are based on falsehood. Man is the deity! Man is divine. When you bow and worship me you are worshiping the essential deity of all mankind. All who oppose this new unity are a cancer in the flesh of humanity and must be put to death for the greater good of all who remain.*

> *And they worshipped the dragon* [Satan, see 12:9] *which gave power unto the beast* [antichrist]: *and*

they worshipped the beast, saying, Who is like unto the beast? Who is able to make war with him? And there was given unto him a mouth speaking great things and blasphemies; and power was given unto him to continue forty and two months. And he opened his mouth in blasphemy against God, to blaspheme his name, and his tabernacle, and them that dwell in heaven (Rev. 13:4-6).

The Bible says that there will be a time when people will listen to evil spirits. Paul wrote,

Now the Spirit speaketh expressly, that in the latter times some shall depart from the faith, giving heed to seducing spirits, and doctrines of devils (1 Tim. 4:1).

Those who accept the teaching and leading of the deceivers will seek to kill all who follow Christ Jesus.

Many in the New Age movement openly advocate this coming time of purging:

Then shall they deliver you up to be afflicted, and shall kill you: and ye shall be hated of all nations for my name's sake (Matt. 24:9).

When he opened the fifth seal, I saw under the altar the souls of those who had been slain because of the word of God and the testimony they had maintained. They called out in a loud voice, "How long, Sovereign Lord, holy and true, until you judge the inhabitants of the earth and avenge our blood?" Then each of them was given a white robe, and they were told to wait a little longer, until the number of their fellow servants and brothers who were to be killed as they had been was completed (Rev. 6:9-11;NIV).

When Christians are killed, it will not be viewed as a real crime. They will be doing us a "favor." If they purge us, we will be reincarnated so that we can experience a New Age salvation!

The last days will be marked by unrepented sorcery, idolatry, and murder! These are the very sins that the New Age/UFO religion will promote.

The rest of mankind that were not killed by these plagues still did not repent of the work of their hands; they did not stop worshiping demons, and idols of gold, silver, bronze, stone and wood — idols that cannot see or hear or walk. Nor did they repent of their murders, their magic arts, their sexual immorality or their thefts (Rev. 9:20,21;NIV).

Through subjective and deceptive experiences many are accepting the UFO lie. Once convinced, these contactees often become zealous New Age witnesses, converting others. Brad Steiger acknowledges that UFO contactees are often called to be New Age evangelists:

They have become messengers for a new gospel. [8]

There is an enormous amount of New Age revelatory material that has been given to the UFO contactees...[9]

These entities that have been called "space brothers" are teaching New Age ideas to the UFO contactees. The UFO contactee often becomes one of a growing number of New Age advocates, mediums, or messengers that are proclaiming the demonic deception as truth.

UFO SPIRIT ENTITIES TEACH NEW AGE CONCEPTS.

The "space brothers" (demonic deceivers) communicate basic tenants of New Age occultism. Steiger observes,

The Space beings seem very concerned with the spread of what has come to be known as New Age concepts...[10]

Let us now look at some specific ideas and tactics the "space brothers" are using to spread the deceiver message, influence, and control.

KARMA AND REINCARNATION

Karma and reincarnation are foundational concepts of New Age occultism. While rejecting God, the Bible, creation, and final judgment, the New Age offers the doctrine of reincarnation. This provides a hope that one can get better through a cyclical evolution. The way karma is dealt with in the present life determines the quality of the next reincarnation. Occult and meditative techniques are supposed to aid one in working out karma. The ultimate goal is for the soul to return to the impersonal "universal soul," known as nirvana or brahm. Concerned adepts will release such combined psychic force that a world grid of power will be brought into existence. This will force the entire race of mankind into the new perception (paradigm shift). When enough people realize their godhood, this will come to pass. Only the bad seed who resist change will be left out — in fact, eliminated.

Dora Gugliotta was one of the leading initiators for the transcendental meditation movement in Canada. Personally taught in Spain by Maharishi Mahesh Yogi, the founder of TM, she flourished in the movement. One night a Christian called Dora on the phone and quoted three Bible verses to her. That night Dora accepted Christ as her Saviour and immediately withdrew from TM, I Ching, aura balancing, and other forms of occult practices in which she was involved.

She is now an effective witness for Christ. Although employed as a computer systems analyst by the Ontario government, Dora finds time to speak at Christian conferences. She has spoken for several of ours. (Both of the authors sponsor and speak at an annual prophecy conference that convenes each year in the Sheraton Hotel in Springfield, Missouri.)

Dora Gugliotta has related to us that at first the initiates in TM experience a "high." They feel like they are walking on clouds. Karma is fast vanishing; their aura brightens. But inevitably harsh reality crowds in upon them. There are still pressures and troubles, and depression can set in.

When the initiates go to their guru with a complaint, they are told that now it is time for an advance into an inner circle through a refined meditative technique. The real cycle is herein revealed: a high, then doubt, trouble, depression, followed by the new technique and then the whole thing is repeated ... over and over. Dora has observed that many cases of possession took place. The New Testament speaks of those false teachers who promise liberty but lead men into bondage.

The doctrine of reincarnation cannot be reconciled with the Bible. We have reviewed the arguments to the contrary through the years and find no validity in any of them. We would not want to destroy anyone's first amendment rights. You can believe and teach anything you want to, but do not deceive yourself into thinking that reincarnation can be reconciled with biblical Christianity.

Each person is responsible for his own sins. Salvation is a promise to individuals. Our standing before God, either forgiven or condemned, is based on our personal response to the gospel of Jesus Christ. There is only one way of salvation and that is through Jesus Christ. There is only one life in which to accept eternal life. There is no second, or third, or one hundredth chance to get it right. Only one life now and a future judgment later!

In the past God overlooked such ignorance, but now he commands all people everywhere to repent. For he has set a day when he will judge the world with justice by the man he has appointed. He has given proof of this to all men by raising him from the dead (Acts 17:30,31;NIV).

Brad Steiger quotes a UFO spirit entity named Semjase:

"Whether we work for God or against God, it matters not, for we are all God — and our forms preserve our Karmic quest in search of the unmanifest." *["Unmanifest" is a term for nirvana.]* [11]

WHEN MAN IS GOD

Genesis records that at the dawn of human history, Satan, the serpent, preached the "cosmic gospel" to Adam and Eve. "You shall not surely die," (reincarnation) and "you shall be as God" (paradigm shift). There you have it! The same lies have been repeated from the beginning until now. The New Age has nothing new to offer. It is the same ancient error that the first man and woman were exposed to and accepted, thus bringing the calamity of the Fall on the whole human race.

In their own way, the words spoken to Eve by the Serpent were the first science fiction story: "Eat, and with this knowledge you may become God." [12]

Science fiction (with a few exceptions) is wedded to the New Age philosophy. It is the entertainment conduit through which the deceivers' message is affecting the masses.

One contactee Brad Steiger interviewed said the following:

The individual will know what the religions of the Ancient Age have always tried to demonstrate: to be STILL and KNOW that YOU are God! [13]

We have quoted Steiger and a few other New Age spokespersons because of their high profile in the movement and because their books are so easily available to those who want to check the validity of our sources. Steiger gives his personal perspective on the "cosmic gospel." After years of research, interviews, and personal experiences he describes the "new spirituality" of this cosmic message:

As "religion" will be replaced by "spirituality," according to this Aquarian perspective, "God" will be replaced by "spirit." God without will be replaced by God within and will be known as the "Spirit" indwelling within all things. [14]

He is not claiming that God is a personal being such as

the Bible teaches. The god of the New Age/UFO is impersonal — the universal soul, mind, or power — in his "spirit." The New Ager sees each living thing as a part of the universal soul. In other words, we are all a part of God as is the planet Earth, the stars, everything.

This pantheistic (God is everything) view was known to the apostle Paul:

> *The wrath of God is being revealed from heaven against all the godlessness and wickedness of men who suppress the truth by their wickedness, since what may be known about God is plain to them, because God has made it plain to them. For since the creation of the world God's invisible qualities — his eternal power and divine nature — have been clearly seen, being understood from what has been made, so that men are without excuse. For although they knew God, they neither glorified him as God nor gave thanks to him, but their thinking became futile and their foolish hearts were darkened. Although they claimed to be wise, they became fools and exchanged the glory of the immortal God for images made to look like mortal man ... They exchanged the truth of God for a lie, and worshiped and served created things rather than the Creator — who is forever praised...Amen* (Rom. 1:18-32;NIV).

One of Steiger's sources is a "space entity" named Ishkomar channeled through Charles. Charles became a channelor through contact with a UFO. According to Ishkomar men are sovereign. The only authority one must obey is the self in tune with the universal mind!

> *You refuse to accept the fact that your world belongs to all the man beings that inhabit your planet, equally, yet combined as one mind, complete and sovereign.*

> *There can be no ultimate solution to your problems as an individual being or as a sovereign world until you have eliminated the complex barriers you have*

placed between yourselves.

Each of you, singly, is a sovereign being and could be likened to a universe complete unto yourselves. You cohabit your world with other beings who are equally sovereign to themselves.[15]

There is an interesting contradiction in this statement. Each person is sovereign in himself. Yet every other person is sovereign. What if all these little gods try to get their way?

Ishkomar also speaks of universal humanity as being sovereign. Here are ideas projecting universal soul, one-world government, one-world religion, and one-world economy.

PURGING THE EARTH — GETTING RID OF THE BAD SEED

Twentieth century gurus pontificate that Earth is about to make a quantum leap of evolution into a glorious New Age. We are at the transition point between the Age of Pisces and the Age of Aquarius. In the glorious future men will become gods. Paranormal powers will be experienced by each "chosen" person. But first those who resist change must be done away with. Earth has become a living being, a goddess named Gaia. She is in communication with the ascended masters of the hierarchy and will cooperate with them in the coming purging of undesirables. Some say that she will be impregnated by the Sun and a manchild will come to birth. This new man will lead humanity into world government and world peace. Environmental and social problems will all be solved.

During a period of catastrophe the collective karma of the race will be purged. A space alien, Ox-Ho, told Steiger this:

People of Earth, you are becoming fourth dimensional whether you are ready or not. Leave the old to those who cling to the old. Don't let the New Age leave you behind.

...Earth must be cleansed. There can be no transition into a new dimension without this cleansing.

The world right now is feeling the effect of the Karmic pattern of the Atlantean culture...[16]

Steiger's summary of the cosmic gospel is worth repeating here:

Man stands now in the transitional period before the dawn of a New Age. With peace, love, understanding, and brotherhood on man's part, he will see a great new era begin to dawn.

If man should not raise his vibratory rate within a set period of time, severe Earth changes and major cataclysms will take place. Such disasters will not end the world, but shall serve as cataclysmic crucibles to burn off the dross of unreceptive humanity. Those who die in such dreadful purgings will be allowed to reincarnate on higher levels of development so that their salvation will be more readily accomplished.[17]

The claim is that the coming New Age is irreversible. The fact is that it isn't irreversible. Rather, it will be unsuccessful and short lived. For only seven years does the "wilfull king" or Antichrist preside over a New Age. On the other hand God's kingdom is eternal. It will never end!

But the judgment shall sit, and they shall take away his dominion, to consume and to destroy it unto the end. And the kingdom and dominion, and the greatness of the kingdom under the whole heaven, shall be given to the people of the saints of the most High, whose kingdom is an everlasting kingdom, and all dominions shall serve and obey him (Dan. 7:26,27).

THE NEW HUMANITY — DARWIN'S DREAM FULFILLED?

After this "purging" a new age and a new humanity will supposedly emerge. Mankind is being promised this new existence if he will only follow the leadership and the teachings of his "space brothers." Another of Brad Steiger's contacts, Sut-Ko, told him,

Many of your peoples are now aligning their consciousness with the realities of the inner world...

...Change with which Earthman must align or perish.[18]

Sut-Ko added this:

Your peoples have to undergo changes of consciousness, and at this time, only those whose consciousness is attuned with the things of a new dispensation will take into themselves, their beings, the increased energies and use these for their future transitional move.[19]

What is the new consciousness the deceivers are promising New Age/UFO believers? The new enhanced consciousness for some is probably demon possession; for all, bondage and control. People are inviting demons into their lives. As quoted earlier they will "take into themselves, these beings..." They are relinquishing control to the deceivers. They experience emotions that make it seem that a new source of energy flows from the wellspring of the divine within.

As for the UFO experience, demons are fully capable of materializations and illusions for deceptive purposes. They can telepathically project images in the minds of contactees, stirring up feelings that reinforce the deception.

ONE WORLD — ONE RELIGION

One of the alien communicators advocates tearing down all the walls of separation between peoples and nations.

...and this is what the races must do. They must become one person.

I see that there will be one major world religion...[20]

This sounds very nice, so kind and peaceful, but behind it is tyranny. Since Bible Christianity makes exclusivist claims we become the enemy. But it is the nature of our faith that any compromise on this point is rebellion against our Lord who said, "He that is not with me is against me." The New Age demands an unacceptable compromise that would result in a denial of our faith. New Age style unity is not an option for Bible-believing Christians. That is why we are branded as the "bad seed" slated for extinction. The New Age religion is tyrannical because it will not allow us to believe as we must. In spite of their precept that each person is entitled to his own reality, it seems that our reality is the only one intolerable to them. Saying that they are for peace, they are ready to murder us for our evangelical faith.

Ruth Montgomery adds another dimension:

Everyone is from God, or consciousness. Everyone on Earth is actually a space being, but no one comes from outer space. Really we come from inner space. All that we are, are thoughts.[21]

The prophet Isaiah thundered out the Words of the Almighty:

I am the Lord, and there is none else, there is no God beside me ... That they may know from the rising of the sun, and from the west, that there is none beside me. I am the Lord, and there is none else ... For thus saith the Lord that created the heavens; God himself that formed the earth and made it; he hath established it, he created it not in vain, he formed it to be inhabited: I am the Lord; and there is none else ... And there is no God else beside me; a just God and a Saviour; there is none beside me (Isa. 45:5,6,18,21).

God is personal, loving, forgiving, holy, and just. He is no illusion. He is THE reference point for all things because all things were made by Him and are sustained by Him. He is the God who promises an eternal future of joy in His kingdom!

PSYCHIC PHENOMENA

UFO appearances and contacts manifest various kinds of paranormal or psychic phenomena.

...Brian Scott case (five occasions, Arizona and California, 1971-75) ... he regularly enters spontaneous trance states in which he produces automatic writing and computer perfect automatic drawings ... Scott is being used as a channel to reveal the following: secrets of cloning and genetic engineering for all mankind to use; machines operating on the principle of quantum displacement physics, which will enable mankind to transport matter across space and through time; and last, but by no means least, the design for a "free psychic energy machine," which would enable all mankind to have the same thought at the same moment.[22]

Uri Geller ... and his psychic sidekick, Dr. Andrija Puharich, say they are in contact with "The Nine," a cabal of extraterrestrials who hail from the planet Hoova. The Nine claim to have solved all the problems of existence and have come to teach the people of the Earth a "new science" which features teleportation (transfer of material objects from one place to another), transmutation of matter, control over biological systems, and implantation of feelings and experiences into people's minds. It should be noted that his "new science" is in fact the old occult; all of these spirit-induced phenomena are well known to occult and psychic practitioners from time immemorial.[23]

The devil is still using the same bag of tricks to deceive

mankind. It is obvious from the duplication of phenomena that UFOs are part of the old occult/psychic domain.

MOTHER GODDESS, GAIA

As mentioned earlier Gaia is the New Age goddess. She is said to be the living planet Earth. There is a lot of the Gaia cult in the environmentalist movement. Ted Turner's "Captain Planet" cartoon series for children exploits her. We must protect and care for this earth. This is God's own mandate to us. Do your part for the environment, but be wary of the New Age connections in the movement. Space beings (actually the deceivers) tell us that the planet is a living entity. Steiger writes,

> *Within the past sixteen years, there has been an increasing number of reports concerning the appearance of a Great Mother image ... Are we witnessing the activation of a long slumbering Goddess...* [24]

> *...the New Age proposes that the earth is literally a living entity. She is the Green Goddess, a fertility deity.* [25]

The earth is a created thing, not a living entity. Earth supports life. It was created to do so. But it is not alive. It is not to be worshiped.

UFO CONTACTEES RESIST BIBLE TRUTH

They are not unbiased. Everyone is entitled to their own reality as long as it is not Bible Christianity. To be a part of the New Age one must reject Bible truth.

> *Very often UFO contactees are, by their admission, individuals who have become disillusioned with the existing religious institutions.* [26]

These individuals are not unbiased objective researchers. They are pro-occult, anti-biblical in faith. In fact one of the early leading promoters of the UFO religion was involved in occult practices before his theories were formed. Von Daniken himself has stated that the theory came to him on an astral trip and that he knows himself to be a reincarnated ancient astronaut.[27] We remind you that von Daniken wanted this theory to become a new religion that would replace Christianity, against which he has great animosity.

In addition to the contactees' bias against Christianity, the entities themselves promote this hatred for anything biblical. One spirit guide rebuked a person who was mixing in too much Bible with her psychic revelations. Ruth Montgomery writes,

> *The Guides responded: "She would be wise not to infuse so much biblical religion into her messages, as the Ashtar Command is nondenominational and, like all spacebeings, worships the one Creator of us all. She is not hearing from the ones you mention,"* (Authors' note: the persons she is referring to are *Jesus, Mary, and other saints) "but is feeling what they might have conveyed. We don't like to see the issue unduly tied in with biblical stories...*[28]

"For the time will come when men will not put up with sound doctrine. Instead, to suit their own desires, they will gather around them a great number of teachers to say what their itching ears want to hear. They will turn their ears away from the truth and turn aside to myths" (2 Tim. 4:3,4;NIV).

Now let us take a closer look at the claims of Shirley MacLaine, a leading spokesperson for the New Age and the UFO phenomena.

SHIRLEY MACLAINE AND THE UFO CONNECTION

Shirley MacLaine is a bright person with a vivacious personality. She is an interesting, articulate, talented, nice person. It is not our intention to portray her as some kind of monster. In fact we pray daily for her Christian enlightenment. What a powerful witness she could be for Jesus, when she comes to know Him. Bear in mind that the New Agers are not our enemies. They are souls who need our Lord. Her belief in UFOs and ETIs is an important part of her overall New Age religion. She has dabbled in many forms of occult activity. Here is a comment about her book *Out On A Limb:*

Shirley MacLaine believes in reincarnation, karma, communication with astral-plane entities through psychic mediums, UFOs, and extraterrestrials, all based solely on subjective experience.[29]

She was already deeply involved in occultic practices by the time she began to encounter the realm of UFOs and ETIs. The following is an excerpt from a conversation she had with John, a channeled spirit:

"...There were extraterrestrials visiting this planet then, as now."
(SM)"...Are you saying that we have had outer space visitations since the beginning of time?"
"That is correct..."
(SM)"...what kind of knowledge were these extraterrestrials bringing?"
John answered immediately. "The only important knowledge is the spiritual knowledge of God within man..."[30]

This next excerpt concerns the concept of God:

(SM)"Okay." I said, "but what do you call God?"
"God or the God Force, of which all things are a part," said John, "is the Divine energy..."[31]

Notice that ETIs are linked with the occultic teaching of the universal soul, a New Age teaching.

The UFO deception is related to all that follows in this narrative. Their supposed ancient contact with man is designed to give credibility to all that follows. The point is that the New Age teaching is claimed to be part of an unbroken thread of revelation that encompasses not only ancient Earth religions but even religions from outer space! This fallacy looks good until one asks the question, "Are UFOs real?" We have demonstrated in this book that they are real but are not what they are claimed to be. They are materializations produced by demonic energy, or in some cases they are the product of hypnotic illusions. Their purpose is deception. That is why we call the aliens deceivers.

From this John went on to tell her that the Bible was unreliable, that it was reinterpreted:

> *(SM)"Isn't the Bible supposed to be the Word of God?"*
> *"Yes, in the main it is. Although much of what exists in your Bible today has been reinterpreted."* [32]

John claimed that men of ill will reinterpreted the Bible to hide the truth of reincarnation and man's divinity.

> *"The real truth being the process of each soul's progression through the ages. The real truth being each soul's responsibility for its own behavior in the realization of its own divinity."*
> *(SM)"You mean reincarnation?"*
> *"That is correct..."* [33]

Shirley MacLaine describes the long spiritual pilgrimage she has followed. It has led her to believe in the ancient astronaut idea, theories about Atlantis, the lost continent, trance mediumship, personal godhood. In her book *Out on a Limb* and in the television documentary she is seen with guru David standing on the seashore. Both are exulting, "I am God. I am God. I am God."

Near the end of the book she is told that she has been selected to go and preach this New Age faith. How does she receive her calling? An ETI named Mayan has selected her and relates this through her guru friend David:

> *"...Then Mayan had to convince me. And now I*

have to convince you..." "What it comes down to,
Shirley, is that you're to be a teacher. Like me. But on
a much wider scale." [34]

She was not fully convinced. David encourages her that
she will not be looked upon as a kook, but will find that
people will accept her teaching.

" ... was I now supposed to write an account of my past
lives, God, and extraterrestrials? I laughed at the logical
absurdity of it."

"...Everyone is motivated by a desire to know the truth.
Everyone."

"The truth? What truth?"

"The simple truth," he said, "of knowing yourself. And to
know yourself is to know God." [35]

The result of her encounter with the New Age, UFOs
and ETIs is well known. She has become a world-wide
spokesperson for the New Age. We do not know if recent
reports that she is rethinking the whole involvement and
even considering Jesus are accurate. We have been praying
for her a long time. We hope.

Dr. LaGard Smith writes,

> *We become ripe for paranormal exploitation, and it*
> *is there that Shirley MacLaine takes us — to a*
> *Twilight Zone of curiosity filled with mystics,*
> *mediums, trance-channeling, deja vu, ESP, and*
> *UFOs.*
>
> *Before launching off into a world of speculation*
> *about the various strange phenomena that are said to*
> *support the notion of reincarnation, there is this to*
> *consider: UFOs are fun to talk about until they are*
> *used to support a pervasive philosophy of life. Are we*
> *willing to risk the destiny of our eternal existence on*
> *a belief in flying saucers? Deja vu is interesting and*
> *ESP is intriguing, but do they give us any assurance*
> *that we have more than one life to live? Mediums may*
> *be faddish and psychics may be the latest craze, but*
> *where are they leading us? To a meaningful life and*

afterlife, or to spiritual disaster? [36]

"Prove all things; hold fast that which is good" (1 Thess. 5:21,22).

Yea, let God be true, but every man a liar (Rom. 3:4).

FOOTNOTES

[1]Dr. Clifford Wilson, "UFOs and Their Missions Impossible," *Word of Truth,* p,161.

[2]Randall N. Baer, *Inside the New Age Nightmare,* Huntington House, pp.145-146.

[3]Shirley MacLaine, *Out on a Limb,* p.352.

[4]Wanda Marrs, *New Age Lies to Women,* Living Truth Publications, p.197.

[5]Texe Marrs, *Texe Marrs Book of New Age Cults and Religions,* Living Truth Publications, p.63.

[6]Ibid., p.96.

[7]Brad Steiger, *Revelation: The Divine Fire,* A Berkley Book, pp.157-158.

[8]Brad Steiger, *The Fellowship,* Ivy Books, p.39.

[9]Ibid., p.40.

[10]Ibid., p.55.

[11]Ibid., p.38.

[12]*SCP Journal,* August 1977, Vol.1 No.2, "The Modern Prometheus: Science Fiction and the New Consciousness," p.8.

[13]Brad Steiger, *The Fellowship,* Ivy Books, p.183.

[14]Ibid., p.186.

[15]Brad Steiger, *Revelation: The Divine Fire,* A Berkley Book, p.145.

[16]Ibid., p.204.

[17]Ibid., p.158.

[18]Ibid., p.205.

[19]Ibid., p.206.

[20]Ibid., p.207. Revelations given through a channelor named Melanie.

[21]Ruth Montgomery, *Aliens Among Us,* Fawcett/Crest, p.163.

[22]*SCP Journal,* August 1977, Vol.1 No.2, "UFOs — Is Science Fiction Coming True?" p.18.

[23]Ibid.

[24]Brad Steiger, *The Fellowship,* Ivy Books, p.29.

[25]Wanda Marrs, *New Age Lies to Women,* Living Truth Publications, p.134.

[26]Brad Steiger, *The Fellowship,* Ivy Books, p.39.

[27]Ibid., p.64.

[28]Ruth Montgomery, *Aliens Among Us,* Fawcett/Crest, p.44.

[29]Dr. F. LaGard Smith, *Out On a Broken Limb,* Harvest House, p.12.

[30]Shirley MacLaine, *Out on a Limb,* p.202, a channeled spirit, John, is speaking to SM.

[31]Ibid., p.204.

[32]Ibid.

[33]Ibid.

[34]Ibid., p.312, David reveals to SM that she is called by an ETI named Mayan to teach the New Age message.

[35]Ibid., pp.312-313.

[36]Dr. F. LaGard Smith, *Out On a Broken Limb,* Harvest House, p.40.

CHAPTER TWELVE

TO GO WHERE NO MAN HAS GONE BEFORE

THE GREAT DISAPPEARANCE

Near where I live there is a fine Italian restaurant. It sits isolated on a hilltop. Suppose you and I and a few of our friends are having a lovely dinner there. Suddenly our group, along with the other seventy-one people in the Villa Rosarita, disappears. No one else in the world vanishes, just the folks in the restaurant. Imagine what the headlines will look like on the day following the mysterious disappearance of over seventy people. Gone without a trace! Is this a new Bermuda Triangle?

One Sunday evening you are sitting in church along with about two hundred other people. Suddenly everyone vanishes. No one else in the world is disappearing, just those in that one church. (This is not the rapture. We are portraying an imaginary event.) By midnight that night, who would be worried about you? Who would wonder where you are? "Why hasn't she come home?" "Where is he?" "What could have happened to them?" By 2 a.m. how many calls will the local and state police receive? How many missing persons reports will be filed by 6 a.m.?

As dawn approaches you can imagine the scene around

the church, now cordoned off by police barricades. Investigation has begun. Where did they go? Local newspaper and television reporters are on the scene, pressing the police investigators for details. Who is missing? How could this happen? Where are they?

By noon television crews from all over the USA and Canada have set up shop. Hot dog vendors have set up their stands to serve the needs of the growing crowd of curious onlookers and investigative reporters. People from "Current Affair," "Hard Copy," and "Unsolved Mysteries" are there. There is so little information that the reporters start interviewing each other on camera, trading theories. Look! There is Peter Jennings, and Bob Simons talking to Mike Wallace. I hear Larry King has just arrived. Before nightfall television crews from London, Paris, Mexico City, Toronto, Rome, Moscow, Hong Kong, and a score of other nations are on the scene.

This is the biggest news of the century. Nothing like this has ever happened before, or has it?

"Yes," someone recalls, "it has happened before." Remember the sailing ship *Mary Celeste*? In the last century the *Mary Celeste* was found adrift with no sign of its crew or passengers. They were simply gone. There was an adequate supply of food and water on board and the ship was not damaged. There was no evidence of any struggle or other emergency. Everything appeared normal, except that there were no longer any people aboard!

Entire books have been written about the *Mary Celeste*. Almost every month some new book about strange disappearances is published. They usually include a chapter about the *Mary Celeste*. Frequently there are magazine articles that recount the strange events surrounding the *Mary Celeste*. People are fascinated, and some strangely are disturbed by this unexplained occurrence, the disappearance of just a few people.

The stories about people disappearing from a restaurant and a church are imaginary. The story of the *Mary Celeste* is true. But one day a disappearance is really going to happen on a scale so big as to be almost unimaginable. It will shake this world to its very foundations. Billions of people will be in a state of shock.

THE RAPTURE OF THE CHURCH

One day, we estimate, about 500 million born-again Christians will vanish off the face of planet Earth. This is the catching away or rapture of the Church. The word "rapture" does not appear in the King James authorized translation of the Bible. However its equivalent is in the original Greek text of the New Testament.

For the Lord himself shall descend from heaven with a shout, with the voice of the archangel, and with the trump of God: and the dead in Christ shall rise first: Then we which are alive and remain shall be caught up together with them in the clouds, to meet the Lord in the air: and so shall we ever be with the Lord. Wherefore comfort one another with these words (1 Thess. 4:16-18).

RAPTURE: A BIBLICAL WORD — EXAMINING THE ORIGINAL GREEK TEXT

The Greek word "harpazo" is translated "caught up" in verse 17 of the authorized English King James translation. The Latin Vulgate, an early translation from the Greek, uses the word "rapio." The English word rapture is a direct translation of the Greek harpazo and the Latin rapio. "Caught up" is barely an adequate translation of harpazo. In fact it is a pale translation and does not reflect the richness of the word harpazo. Harpazo is better translated "caught away forcefully in a state of ecstasy."

The word "harpazo" is variously translated in the KJV as "Take it by force" (Matt. 11:12); "Take him by force" (John 6:15); "pluck" (John 10:28,29). In Acts 8:39 we read that the Spirit of God "caught away Philip." Philip the evangelist was literally moved by the Spirit from one location to another. This accompanies the account of his witness to and the subsequent conversion of the Ethiopian eunuch. The apostle Paul was "caught up to the third heaven" and "caught up into paradise" (2 Cor. 12:2,4). In the last book of the Bible the manchild (most understand this to be a retrospective view of Jesus' ascension.) being "caught up unto God" (Rev. 12:5). All of these passages use the Greek word "harpazo." From this we derive an understanding of the full meaning of the word. Rapture is the best one word translation available in the English language for harpazo.

Jesus had promised His followers that He would return and receive them unto himself so that they could be in paradise, the third heaven. That is where Jesus is now. Following His death, resurrection, and ascension He is seated at the right hand of the Father. He is active and doing things to prepare for our future.

One day, Jesus was talking to the twelve disciples. He said, "Little children, yet a little while I am with you. Ye shall seek me: and as I said unto the Jews, Whither I go, ye cannot come..."

Simon Peter said unto him, "Lord, whither goest thou?"

Jesus answered him, "Whither I go, thou canst not follow me now; but thou shalt follow me afterwards" (John 13:33,36).

"Let not your heart be troubled: ye believe in God, believe also in me. In my Father's house are many mansions: if it were not so, I would have told you. I go to prepare a place for you. And if I go and prepare a place for you, I will come again, and receive you unto myself; that where I am, there ye may be also" (John 14:1-3).

Jesus said that He was leaving. They wondered how they would get to where He was going. He replied that He would come back and get them ("receive you unto myself") and take them there to be with Him. Many other passages in 2 Thessalonians, 1 Corinthians 15, and so on refer to the great Rapture event.

WHEN MILLIONS VANISH — YOU CAN FORGET THE *MARY CELESTE*

We estimate that there are probably about 500 million born-again Christians living on Earth right now. That figure is based on statistics furnished by various evangelical denominations and missions organizations. The actual number does not matter, but it is going to be a significant amount. Every person whom God recognizes as a born-again believer will be taken in the Rapture. Religious hypocrites and pretenders will not go. Church membership is no guarantee. At the judgment seat of Christ only believers appear to receive their rewards for service, following their born-again experience. We are not saved by works, but when converted to Christ we are to work in His kingdom. Our works will be evaluated. Some receive great reward, some little. (See 1 Cor. 3:1-15.)

When half a billion people mysteriously vanish from this planet, pandemonium will break loose! The wildest of speculations will run rampant.

For a while there will be only one possible topic of conversation! Talk show hosts will bring in top scientific experts, psychologists, political commentators, and religious leaders. Somebody has to have an answer! The world is reeling in shock. What does it mean? How could it happen? Where have they gone? Will we ever see them again? Could it happen to me? Fear mounts. Panic is rampant. Some elements of society turn to violence, vandalism, and looting as never before.

Joint presidential and congressional commissions will be organized; top scientists will collect data; religious leaders will consult each other; heads-of-state will be in conference. Someone must come up with an answer. Fears of the unknown must be salved for the general populace. Many who are even now a part of the New Age movement will ponder possible paranormal phenomena as the answer. Of course the "alien invader" concept will be among the answers considered. We think it will quickly come to the forefront.

The apostle John wrote the Book of Revelation while in exile on the Island of Patmos. Following his being caught up into the heavenlies, in a vision, he saw the dark days that would fall on Earth. The time he saw was a seven year period known as the great global trauma or the Tribulation.

And the kings of the earth, and the great men, and the rich men, and the chief captains, and the mighty men, and every bondman, and every free man, hid themselves in the dens and in the rocks of the mountains; And said to the mountains and rocks, Fall on us, and hide us from the face of him that sitteth on the throne, and from the wrath of the Lamb: For the great day of his wrath is come; and who shall be able to stand? (Rev. 6:15-17).

It is not likely that most of the beleaguered residents of the world will believe the truth. One can hardly imagine their saying, "Oh my, those evangelical Christians were right after all. Jesus came back like they said He would and took them all to heaven. Now we wretched sinners are left behind to face the wrath of God." Not likely!

Knowing this first, that there shall come in the last days scoffers, walking after their own lusts, And saying, Where is the promise of his coming? (2 Pet. 3:3).

144,000 WHO KNOW THE TRUTH — SOME EXCEPTIONS NOTED

Early in the seven years of trouble 144,000 people, 12,000 from every tribe of Israel (Rev. 7) will call on Christ. They are sealed unto salvation and service. They become mighty witnesses. They are the first to call on God early in the Tribulation, but following their witness, a multitude will find the Lord Jesus Christ. They will know and declare the truth about what has happened. This enrages the leaders of the nations. They attempt to kill as many of these people as possible. The converts to Christ, like those who have taken leave of planet Earth, are labeled "bad seed." They must be exterminated.

There will be twenty-one judgments poured out on Earth during the time of trouble. They are labeled the judgments of the opening of the seven seals, the sounding of the seven trumpets, and the outpouring of the seven vials (bowls) of wrath! The twenty-one judgments of the Tribulation, described in Revelation 6-16 seem like a fulfillment of the New Age predictions of a time of distress that they foresee preceding their "dawning of the Age of Aquarius." How close to the truth, yet how far away!

LIVE FROM BRUSSELS

It is inevitable that scientists, social analysts, religious leaders, and politicians will come up with a joint statement. One evening all television and radio programs are interrupted:

We interrupt your regular broadcast for this special news break from Brussels. We take you live to the United Planetary Commission headquarters. Spokesperson Shandra Shambala is about to make an important announcement.

Greetings to all mankind. We address ourselves to all men and women of goodwill on all continents. These are difficult and stressful times. After deliberation by a majority of the heads of nations it is agreed that circumstances demand that the United Planetary Commission and the United Nations must now become an international federation with one central government for the entire planet. Brussels, Rome, and New York are being considered as possible sites for the capitol for the United Federation of Mankind (UFM). A leader has fortunately been chosen who has such unusual qualifications that it is agreed by all of your presidents, premiers, and kings that no one else could even be considered for the position. In effect we are now announcing the New World Order. It will be called the United Federation of Mankind. Ten European nations have already united and will provide a model for the UFM.

Earth has been invaded by hostile aliens. Millions of our people have been kidnaped. Some fantasized at first that they were taken for intergalactic zoos. Some even thought that the aliens might have taken them for a protein food supply. We now know the answer and it is even worse than imagined. There is no longer any question that the nations of Earth must unite and form one federated government. After centuries of striving fruitlessly for this unity we now realize that it is the one hope in the midst of the chaos that has befallen us.

For the sake of mutual survival we have taken the first steps toward the uniting of all nations under one government. Benevolent aliens, who have shown themselves to us and have communicated with us will assist us. They have selected a human person whom they have endowed with supernormal wisdom and power. He will seem like a miracle worker. He will have powers no man has ever had. He will lead us to world peace. Meanwhile it is essential that we organize an adequate defense force to protect ourselves from further interplanetary threats. All Earth's resources and technologies must be used to this end.

The appalling truth has finally been realized. The hostile aliens have taken millions of our people for a sinister purpose. The hostiles want to take over our planet, but they want to minimize their risks in the forthcoming invasion. Our human brothers and sisters are right now being reprogrammed. Hostile aliens have kidnaped the missing persons for the purpose of genetic, electronic, and psychological engineering. They are being made into android-like slaves who will obey the commands of their new masters. They will be back, as the vanguard of the alien invasion. For those of you who may have tuned in late, let me repeat: After a thorough investigation, conducted by Earth's greatest scientists and analysts, we are convinced that this planet has been attacked by aliens from another star system. Our evidence indicates that we can expect a return of these alien invaders together with their programed shock troops in an effort to take over our planet. Meanwhile we can expect a series of attacks upon the planetary ecosystem. They will use advanced technological methods of manipulating the environment. Our new allies, representatives of the Ascended Masters of the Hierarchy have informed us that the rebel aliens are capable of doing this. They will try to devastate the planet and weaken us before their attempted takeover. We must now unite to prepare for this coming struggle. Together humanity along with our new friends can resist these invaders. It will require the full cooperation of every citizen. Dissidents must be dealt with severely: they will be executed. If the dissident problem becomes too great we will be forced to resort to harsher measures. Public executions by guillotine, gallows and the electric chair will be reinstituted. It will be the duty of each world citizen to report subversives. Nothing will be allowed to impede our efforts to insure survival.

The troublesome nations of the Middle East, especially Israel, must be brought into conformity with the larger goals of mankind. No more ideas about a certain nation, race, or people being an exclusively and divinely "chosen" group can be tolerated. We have proposed a seven year agreement which the Middle East nations will be required to sign and abide by. National boundaries will finally be established and maintained. At the end of the seven years renegotiation will be considered. Any nation dissenting will simply have to be destroyed. Israel, long the darling of the West, must give up its recalcitrant behavior and conform to our new world vision. We at the UPC and the UN are aware that the Israelis, long pampered by America, have built up an arsenal of high-tech weapons. They even have secret weapons about which we have little information. We are so determined to solve the Middle East problem, that if it becomes necessary we will require every nation of the world to send armies to the Middle East and take it over for the greater good of United Mankind.

The alien invasion and loss of millions of our people is a traumatic event. However, we ask all of you to be strong and to find within yourselves the spiritual resources to overcome your fears. The awakening god-force in all people will lead us past this momentary crisis into a glorious New World Order. As bad as the events of the last few weeks have been, we in the UPC are confident that in coming years, historians will see this era as the time when humanity finally united and we began realizing our full potential together! Good night and may the god-force in all of us fill our lives with peace!

DELUSION, TRUTH, AND ERROR

Satan always deludes by using a mixture of truth and error. We are leaving, but not to be enslaved. We will be liberated, endowed with incredible powers and capabilities in our resurrected and glorified bodies. The Bible says that we will be like Christ and have a body "like unto the glorious body of His resurrection." We will be "reprogrammed," not to be slaves, but to be freed from the slavery we now experience in our limited present state. We will forever be free from the slavery of sin, liberated in the Rapture. The apostle Paul wrote, "we shall all be changed, In a moment, in the twinkling of an eye, at the last trump: for the trumpet shall sound, and the dead shall be raised incorruptible, and we shall be changed" (1 Cor. 15:51,52). "For the creation waits with eager longing for the revealing of the sons of God" (Romans 8:19;RSV). These mortal bodies shall become indestructible, immortal. Please read the entire fifteenth chapter of 1 Corinthians.

WE ARE COMING BACK!

And we will be back. You can count on it. We will be back, not as shock troops or cannon fodder for an alien invasion. We will accompany Jesus Christ the King of kings and eternal Lord of lords in the hour of His triumph. We will accompany Him as witnesses to His victory over the Antichrist and all the hordes of hell.

Jesus will defeat the armies of the beast, not with physical force or weapons, but with spiritual power. He does not need to use us as shock troops. Paul prophesied of Christ's victory over the wicked son of perdition, the Antichrist. "And then shall that Wicked be revealed, whom the Lord shall consume with the spirit of his mouth, and shall destroy with the brightness of his coming" (2 Thess. 2:8). Read Revelation 19 for a broader view of the heavenly liberation of planet Earth.

ARMAGEDDON WHY? — NO DOOMSDAY AFTER ALL

When Jesus defeats the 200 million men army of the Beast (Antichrist) at Armageddon (Rev. 16 and 19), it is not an act of wanton slaughter. Revelation tells us that Jesus returns to destroy those who have the power to destroy Earth (See Rev. 11:18). The Beast's army will have powerful doomsday weapons (they already exist) that could bring an end to all life on Earth. That is Satan's goal — the destruction of all humanity. Christ destroys the Earth destroyers to preserve humanity. He is not coming back to destroy the Earth but to preserve it.

We are not looking for the end of the world. We are looking for a new beginning under the benevolent rulership of Jesus Christ. In Revelation the Almighty announces, "BEHOLD I MAKE ALL THINGS NEW" (Rev. 21:5). Those who have responded to the message of the 144,000 witnesses and have escaped martyrdom will rebuild and repopulate the Earth during the thousand year millennium. The raptured and glorified Church will be here to work with Jesus in administrative, religious teaching, and governing capacities to effect a paradise like condition on Earth. After the millennium the heavens and Earth will be renovated and there will be a New Heaven and a New Earth. That is the eternal state.

EVEN NOW THEY HATE THE RAPTURE!

Many people today know about and literally despise the Rapture idea. We cannot bow to their blind hatred. The Rapture idea is important to us as a present spiritual shield of protection, even before its actual fulfillment as an event. For one thing, if people believe in the Rapture, no false christ can ever delude them, in this Church age. If someone is said to be "the Christ," we know it is impossible. When the real Jesus comes, we will "rise to meet Him in the air." The concept is as important as the event, for it is God's insurance against the delusions of the false christs.

One New Age writer says that if the Evangelicals, Pentecostals, and Charismatics want to be a part of the New Age movement, they are going to have to get rid of that tired, old, worn out doctrine, the rapture of the Church. Lincoln, Leigh, and Baigent, authors of the books *Holy Blood, Holy Grail* and *The Messianic Legacy,* go to every length to ridicule and scoff at the Rapture concept. Perhaps, now, we can see why. Peter Lemesurier in his book *The Armageddon Script* clearly says it is time to stop wasting all the spiritual energy that is spent in anticipation of Christ's return. His book, published by Saint Martin's press in New York, outlines how the New Age can stage a dramatized "second coming" of Christ, satisfy the longing of millions and get on with the program for the New Age.

Does it seem too far-fetched to say those left behind will interpret the Rapture as an alien invasion? It isn't. Ruth Montgomery, writes the following astounding passage in her book *Aliens Among Us:*

> *Although most Earthlings will lose their physical*

lives when the earth shifts on its axis at the close of this century, a good number of enlightened ones will be evacuated by the galactic fleets and returned to Earth for its rehabilitation.[1]

The Rapture will be explained away with a mix of pseudo-science, New Age religion, and both fabricated as well as misinterpreted evidence that will seem to prove that the Rapture is an alien invasion. Steiger writes,

...these UFO prophets have not only brought God physically to this planet, but they have created a blend of science and religion that offers a theology more applicable to modern mankind.[2]

"Now the Spirit speaketh expressly, that in the latter times some shall depart from the faith, giving heed to seducing spirits, and doctrines of devils" (1 Tim. 4:1-3).

The Space beings seem very concerned with the spread of what has come to be known as New Age concepts...[3]

Believing "the lie" will lead a person to accept the Antichrist as a savior. The Antichrist comes as an "angel of light" when in reality he is a man possessed by the master of the alien deceivers, Lucifer, a fallen angel who intends to destroy us.

THE FOURFOLD DELUSION

The alien UFO perception promotes a four-point delusion. First, it explains away the disappearance of millions of people, the rapture of the Church. Second, it calls all men to unite in a New World Order against a common enemy. Third, it presents man with a "messiah, a savior" (Antichrist). Fourth, it hardens men in their antagonism toward Jesus so they will fight against Him when He returns to Earth. They will think they are fighting the alien invader.

CONFLICT OF THE AGES

After what has emerged following the events of the First Gulf War, can anyone doubt that the disappearance of millions of people will cause the nations to pursue establishment of a world government with renewed fervor? One UFO-logist writes,

> *The battle for the Earth is a spiritual struggle but involves mighty temporal events...*[4]

Lemesurier shows that the New Age religion plans to create a false second coming. He clearly describes a plan to have their "christ" seem to descend in clouds to the Mount of Olives.

> *He will appear in white, shining robes with some of his followers. He will march into Jerusalem and on to the Temple mount. Television will give this false Second Coming worldwide, simultaneous coverage! The Antichrist will display lying wonders to deceive if possible even the elect! So even if famous Church leaders say that it is Jesus, Friend, do not believe them. As long as you haven't been caught up and taken out of this earth to meet the Lord in the air, in a glorified body, you know that it is not the Lord!* [5]

Jesus said there would be false christs (plural). Already some move among us. A man in Chicago proclaims himself as Christ. The Tara Foundation, headed by Benjamin Creme, purchased full-page ads in the *New York Times, USA Today,* and a host of other leading newspapers in many nations to announce that "Christ" materialized a body in the Himalaya Mountains and now resides in London, awaiting His unveiling. A powerful French organization believes its head is a direct physical descendent of Jesus and will rule a revived Roman Empire in the 1990s and the world by the year 2000.

The believer who loves the Lord will not be deceived! We have a sure hope against this deception.

When the real Jesus comes I will know Him — for sure! There will be no doubt about it. When Moses was withstood by the two magicians, Jannes and Jambres, in Pharaoh's court, they could duplicate some of the miracles; but the time came when their powers failed and God triumphed over evil, allowing the children of Israel to leave Egypt in triumph.

One of these days an event will take place that all the forces of hell cannot duplicate nor counterfeit, nor can they stop it. When the trumpet sounds and you are transformed into the likeness of Jesus Christ our Lord, and when you rise to meet Him along with millions of other believers, you will know beyond a shadow of a doubt who you are meeting. It is Jesus! It is the Rapture! Glory to God in the Highest! It is He and not another! This is the real Jesus! [6]

If mankind is convinced that the missing people are taken by aliens with plans for a future invasion and that a messiah has arisen on Earth to save them, most people will readily accept the Antichrist's leadership. Just such a dual idea is already common among UFO advocates. Steiger is a brilliant writer whom we would love to win to our side of this struggle. Please pray for this man who we have no doubt is totally sincere in what he writes:

It would seem from the experiences of certain abductees that the citizens of Earth are encountering at least two representatives of extraterrestrial or multidimensional worlds. There appear to be those UFO intelligences who are genuinely concerned about our welfare and our spiritual and physical evolution, and there are those who seem largely indifferent to our personal needs and our species' longevity. Unless we are somehow perceiving different aspects of the same entities, then it might well be that our beautiful green oasis in space could serve as the prize in a war between worlds. If the Forces of Light and Darkness are about to square off on our turf, humankind could

*find itself the unwilling pawn in the ultimate battle —
the final struggle between Good and Evil.*[7]

Concerning the fear of alien invasion, Steiger further observes that:

*It becomes very frightening to many people to
understand that humankind could be overcome and
even destroyed by programmed men and women from
within the ranks of their species.*[8]

*Assistance on a planetary level will not occur until
all nations put a stop to war. These foolish squabbles
that are going on in the Middle East must cease.
Earth must unite ...* [9]

It is no wonder that people will fight against Christ when He returns at the end of the seven years' great global trauma, the Tribulation. What a tragedy! Those who have accepted the Antichrist as their savior will perish without any hope of forgiveness of their sins. Their quagmire will become deeper and darker with each passing millennia.

THE GREAT ADVENTURE

"Star Trek" has caught the imagination of this generation. Space exploration! We have already reached the moon. What next? "To go where no one has gone before...," But "Star Trek" is only fiction.

There is a much greater adventure waiting the believer in Jesus. This adventure is going to open doors beyond our wildest dreams! We will see things that will astound us and fill us with awe at God's never-ending Universe of wonders. The adventure starts now when we accept Christ as Saviour. It finds its ultimate realization when we are caught up to meet Him. Our trip of an eternal lifetime may be about to begin (we cannot set the exact date). We are going to explore strange new worlds, but we are going on a guided tour with One who has gone before us. We will be accompanied by Jesus, who not only went before, but is the One who created it all! Eternity will continue to unfold the wonders of God's absolutely limitless creation.

Eye hath not seen, nor ear heard, neither have entered into the heart of man, the things which God hath prepared for them that love him. But God hath revealed them unto us by his Spirit: for the Spirit searcheth all things, yea, the deep things of God (1 Cor. 2:9,10).

The apostle John caught a glimpse of the future that awaits us:

And immediately I was in the Spirit: and, behold, a throne was set in heaven, and one sat on the throne. And he that sat was to look upon like a jasper and a sardine stone: and there was a rainbow round about the throne, in sight like unto an emerald. And round about the throne were four and twenty seats: and upon the seats I saw four and twenty elders sitting, clothed in white raiment; and they had on their heads crowns of gold (Rev. 4:1-4).

Friend, are you ready for the great adventure? Put your trust in Jesus who is able to bring redemption to your life and give you a real future, both for now in this world and in the world to come.

But we are bound to give thanks always to God for you, brethren beloved of the Lord, because God hath from the beginning chosen you to salvation through sanctification of the spirit and belief of the truth: Whereunto he called you by our gospel, to the obtaining of the glory of our Lord Jesus Christ (2 Thess. 2:13,14).

We saw earlier that there is a formula that will lead to deception in the last days. There is also a way to insure victory!

Just as there is a formula for delusion and destruction, there is one for victory! What is our safeguard against deception? Love the truth + Believe the truth + Shun unrighteousness = Victory. If you will give yourself to the

Lord, His Word, and yield to the Spirit of God, He will keep you through it all! Where are you right now? If Jesus comes tonight, will you be ready? If persecution and deception prevail in our country, will you stand the test? Now is the opportunity to build a formula for victory in the last days![10]

Behold, what manner of love the Father hath bestowed upon us, that we should be called the sons of God: therefore the world knoweth us not, because it knew him not. Beloved, now are we the sons of God, and it doth not yet appear what we shall be: but we know that, when he shall appear, we shall be like him; for we shall see him as he is. And every man that hath this hope in him purifieth himself, even as he is pure (1 John 3:1-4).

The Lord's invitation to make your reservation for the great adventure is presented to you right now! We hope to see you in the Rapture!

And the Spirit and the bride say, Come. And let him that heareth say, Come. And let him that is athirst come. And whosoever will, let him take the water of life freely. For I testify unto every man that heareth the words of the prophecy of this book, if any man shall add unto these things, God shall add unto him the plagues that are written in this book: And if any man shall take away from the words of the book of this prophecy, God shall take away his part out of the book of life, and out of the holy city, and from the things which are written in this book. He which testifieth these things saith, Surely I come quickly. Amen. Even so, come, Lord Jesus. The grace of our Lord Jesus Christ be with you all. Amen (Rev. 22:17-21).

FOOTNOTES

[1]Ruth Montgomery, *Aliens Among Us,* Fawcett/Crest, p.43

[2]Brad Steiger, *The Fellowship*, Ivy Books, p.1.
[3]Ibid., p.55.
[4]Brad Steiger, *The UFO Abductors*, Berkley Books, p.214, quoting Constable.
[5]Rev. Robert Shreckhise, *I & II Thessalonians, A Practical Study Guide and Commentary*, unpublished.
[6]Dr. David A. Lewis, *Smashing the Gates of Hell*, New Leaf Press, p.61.
[7]Brad Steiger, *The UFO Abductors*, Berkley Books, p.214.
[8]Ibid., p.205.
[9]Brad Steiger, *The Fellowship*, Ivy Books, p.43
[10]Rev, Robert Shreckhise, *I & II Thessalonians, A Practical Study Guide and Commentary*, unpublished.

CHAPTER THIRTEEN

WAR OF THE WORLDS

BETWIXT HEAVEN AND EARTH

In 1957, the year that the European Common Market was founded, Henry Spaak, Belgium's foremost modern statesman, remonstrated,

> *We do not want another committee: we have too many already. What is needed is a man of sufficient stature to hold the allegiance of all people and to lift us out of the economic morass into which we are sinking. Send us such a man and, be he god or devil, we will receive him.*[1]

Mankind is looking for leadership. The world has become so interdependent that old allegiances do not answer the needs of the time in which we live. The economies, ecologies, conflicts, and social upheavals of individual nations are now global concerns. The world is heading for a crisis period of history. There will be increasing global problems and a concurrent increase in the cry of humanity for an answer, for a leader to direct them into an age of peace and prosperity.

Out of the crisis of coming events, one will arise who will gain the allegiance of mankind. He will not be a god or a devil. He will be a man who is totally controlled by the devil. This intriguing and frightening personality, to whom so much research and inquiry has been given, is commonly called the Antichrist.

> *And I saw, and behold a white horse: and he that sat on him had a bow; and a crown was given unto him: and he went forth conquering, and to conquer* (Rev. 6:2).

He will appear on the scene emerging out of a worldwide crisis. The rapture of the Church will be one of the events that speeds the crisis that will launch the Antichrist into center stage of end-time events on Earth. We may have some insight into the leaders of the last days. We may even have very good ideas about the identity of the Antichrist. However, if our hypothesis about the timing of the Rapture (pre-Tribulation) and the subsequent unveiling of the man of sin is true, then the final, positive identification of this person will be withheld until after the Church has departed.

He will not be revealed until after the Rapture because the body of Christ is a restraining force that withholds the final unbridled, satanic onslaught against the human race. Several passages speak of this restraining, resisting ministry of believers:

> *Submit yourselves therefore to God. Resist the devil, and he will flee from you* (James 4:7).

> *Behold, I give unto you power to tread on serpents and scorpions, and over all the power of the enemy: and nothing shall by any means hurt you. Notwithstanding in this rejoice not, that the spirits are subject unto you; but rather rejoice, because your names are written in heaven* (Luke 10:19,20).

> *Let no man deceive you by any means: for that day shall not come, except there come a falling away* (alternate possible translation-departure) *first, and that man of sin be revealed, the son of perdition; Who*

opposeth and exalteth himself above all that is called God, or that is worshipped; so that he as God sitteth in the temple of God, shewing himself that he is God ... And now ye know what withholdeth that he might be revealed in his time. For the mystery of iniquity doth already work: only he who now letteth (restrains) will let (restrain), until he be taken out of the way (2 Thess. 2:3,4, 6,7).

In the chapter on the Rapture, we already looked at verse 3 in 2 Thessalonians, Chapter 2. Taking the thought that we expressed, that the "falling away" refers to the Rapture, and looking at it in context with the other verses (vv. 4, 6,7), we get a picture of events which fit our concept. After the Rapture, when the Restrainer is gone, the man of sin will arise. The identity of the Restrainer is important. We believe that the Restrainer is the Church empowered by the Spirit of God.

CONSIDER THE FOLLOWING:

In verses 6 and 7 Paul speaks of One who restrains the power of iniquity in this present season. The word "letteth" means to restrain. The Elizabethan English of the King James Version often means something different from modern English. There are various views of who is the Withholder or Restrainer. The Withholder will be taken away so that the man of sin can be revealed. Then who is the Withholder? The different views I am aware of are: 1) Law of God, 2) a person, 3) the Spirit, 4) the Church. (The idea of a single person being the Restrainer is just not found anywhere in the Bible so we will not even discuss it.)

Consider for a moment what this Withholder does. He holds back but does not completely overcome the power of iniquity. The Law does this but only to the extent that the Spirit of God convicts men successfully to obey it. The Spirit of God obviously has a part in restraining evil on the earth by this same convicting power. But the Spirit of God has always been in the

*world because He is omnipresent. How can the
omnipresent Spirit be removed? How will the
Tribulation believers come to salvation without His
work, because no man can come to the Father unless
the Spirit draws him to the Father? However, His
special presence has been in the Church. The Church
is salt and light. Salt preserves from decay and light
exposes the deeds of darkness. My opinion is that the
Restrainer is the Spirit-filled church of God through
whom the Lord ministers salt and light in a decaying
world using the power of the Word of God and the
anointing of the Spirit. Even though the Church is the
bride of Christ, a feminine gender, the Church is also
spoken of in masculine, military terms. So the Church
in its masculine role of a restraining army of saints
fits this passage. If this is true, then this means that
the Church will leave the scene before the man of sin
rises to absolute power. We may have an idea of his
identity. He may even be a prominent national ruler
somewhere. There may be persecution and trouble for
the Church. Segments of the Church may even suffer
under him for a time before the Rapture! But it is after
the Withholder or Restrainer is removed that the man
of sin is revealed in all of his wickedness and satanic
power! Then all hell breaks loose on Earth!*[2]

Once we are gone, the restraining force against evil is
lifted. Then begins a great satanic onslaught against
mankind in general, against Israel, and against the
Tribulation saints in particular. Deception such as has
never before been possible will occur in the last days.
Demon possession will flood the earth. Great wars and
catastrophes will rock the planet with satanic blows against
man and God. Out of the turmoil, the Antichrist will arise
to offer man leadership and plausible answers to the
frightening events that the world will be facing. In the
vacuum of truth and leadership that the Rapture will
create, he will ride in like a Saviour on his white horse to
"rescue" man from chaos and destruction.

Steiger speaks of the coming time when mankind will be receptive to this New Age paradigm:

UFO contactees often speak of an impending New Age in which humankind will attain a new consciousness, a new awareness, and a higher state — or frequency — of vibration.[3]

This "new consciousness" is what we would call a reprobate mind, a mind given over to believe the lie of the Antichrist.

It is natural to wonder when this period of time will come to pass. Evidence seems to point to the present era. We do not want to be dogmatic, but never before in the history of mankind has the condition of the world fit so precisely into the picture that prophetic Scriptures described over two millennia ago. For instance, the coming United Europe that is slated in 1992-1993 appears to be close to what Daniel described. In such a setting of history the Antichrist will arise. (Read Dan. 2:40-45; 7:8; 7:19-27; 8:23-25; 11:36-39; and Rev. 13:1-8.)

Out of this new European order a man will arise who will become a powerful political figure. He will also be a powerful psychic who has special endowments from Satan.

The "dark sentences" and "craft" spoken of in these verses speak of the occultic knowledge into which this man is initiated. He will be one given over to the depths of Satan (Rev. 2:24), a man in whom the mystery of iniquity is fully at work (2 Thess. 2:7). He shall practice occult-craft not only for the purpose of deceptive miracles, but for the purpose of destroying all opposition.

In the NIV translation of the Bible, verse 39 of Daniel 11 reads,

He will attack the mightiest fortresses with the help of a foreign god and will greatly honor those who acknowledge him. He will make them rulers over many people and will distribute the land at a price.

This foreign god, the "god of forces" (Dan. 11:38) is

Satan. In the New Age he is called Lucifer, the light bearer. In both the New Age and UFO concepts, he is called the god force, the divine energy. The Bible calls him the dragon, the serpent, Satan, and the devil (see Rev. 20:2). This is the true power behind the Antichrist.

In Revelation, Chapter 13, there are some intriguing statements. Men will worship the dragon, Satan. In the guise of Lucifer, who has been called by one New Age writer the "angel of our evolution," mankind will accept the Antichrist and his "god of forces" as the true persons to be worshipped. The Antichrist will speak blasphemies against God, His name, His tabernacle, and those who dwell in heaven. It is not so hard to see that the Antichrist will blaspheme God and His name. But why the tabernacle and those dwelling in heaven? These relate to the two peoples of God: Israel and the Church.

The earthly people of God, the Jewish remnant, are the objects of Satan's wrath. He will especially hate the new temple that will stand in Jerusalem as the last, earthly, visible hold-out against the Antichrist's influence. He will pollute this temple in an effort to destroy this visible sign of God's promises to the Jewish people. Both Daniel and Jesus spoke of the coming abomination of desolation that will defile the future temple of God. Daniel wrote,

> *And he shall confirm the covenant with many for one week: and in the midst of the week he shall cause the sacrifice and the oblation to cease, and for the overspreading of abominations he shall make it desolate, even until the consummation, and that determined shall be poured upon the desolate* (Dan. 9:27).

Jesus said,

> *When ye therefore shall see the abomination of desolation, spoken of by Daniel the prophet, stand in the holy place, (whoso readeth, let him understand:) Then let them which be in Judaea flee into the mountains: Let him which is on the housetop not come*

down to take any thing out of his house: Neither let him which is in the field return back to take his clothes. And woe unto them that are with child, and to them that give suck in those days! Pray ye that your flight be not in the winter, neither on the Sabbath day: For then shall be great tribulation, such as was not since the beginning of the world to this time, no, nor ever shall be. And except those days should be shortened, there should no flesh be saved: but for the elect's sake those days shall be shortened (Matt. 24:15-22).

The Antichrist will also blaspheme those dwelling in heaven because they are also an unmistakable sign of God's promises. These people are the raptured saints. The Rapture will be a sign of the truth of God's promises that must be distorted if Satan's plan is going to work. In the context of this passage in Revelation Chapter 13 the word "blasphemy" portrays the idea of speaking evil about a holy thing. The question is, what is the character of the blasphemy? Could it in part be that we have been kidnapped by aliens for reprograming in preparation for a coming alien invasion? This is taking a precious promise of God and turning it into an evil scheme of some alien power. It makes the raptured saints out to be an evil force to be opposed. The most terrible thing about such a lie is that is makes our Saviour out to be an arch villain! How Satan loves to take the praise due only to God and to impute to God the condemnation due only to himself! As we have seen before, this not only explains away the Rapture but deceives men concerning the Second Coming. They will be willing to fight Jesus and His heavenly armies because they think they are under alien attack.

The good news is that the Antichrist and Satan will fail! The Antichrist will be destroyed; Satan will be bound. Jesus and His people will reign and enjoy the Millennium and the Eternal Kingdom together, forever!

And he [antichrist] shall plant the tabernacles of

*his palace between the seas in the glorious holy
mountain; yet he shall come to his end, and none shall
help him* (Dan. 11:45).

*But the judgment shall sit, and they shall take
away his dominion, to consume and to destroy it unto
the end. And the kingdom and dominion, and the
greatness of the kingdom under the whole heaven,
shall be given to the people of the saints of the Most
High, whose kingdom is an everlasting kingdom, and
all dominions shall serve and obey him* (Dan. 7:26,27).

This man will arise promising peace. He will promise
answers to the multitude of problems facing mankind,
especially the chaos caused by the Rapture. He will fail
because Satan never intended him to succeed. Satan does
not want mankind to prosper and continue existing. He is
only using the Antichrist and humanity to attempt to
overthrow God himself. Humans, including the Antichrist,
are pawns in Satan's war against heaven. Know this, that
without any doubt, Satan will fail also! Meanwhile, we are
in a battle for souls. Satan's weapon is deception. Our
shield and weapon is truth.

END-TIME MESSENGERS OF DECEPTION

A noted UFO researcher, Jacques Vallee, has stated,

*UFOs and related phenomena are the means
through which man's ideas are being rearranged.*[4]

People have had their thinking rearranged. Only a few
years ago it was the lunatic fringe of society that believed
in aliens from other planets. How the times have changed!
Today, UFOs, close encounters, and New Age thought are
becoming a new pop-theology for those outside the tradition
of biblical faith. Presidents, television and movie stars,
astronauts, scientists, and average citizens are all speaking
about encounters with space-beings. It is out of the closet
and onto the front pages. What is the reason for this
dramatic change in the thinking of so many people?

The change in perceptions about UFOs is not accidental. People in various fields have actively promoted UFO awareness. This has been done in gradual stages until the general world-view has been shifted to accept delusion as truth. At first the idea of UFOs was an oddity. Science fiction books, motion pictures, and television programming played a major role. As people got used to these ideas, they were conveyed in an increasingly favorable light. Now, they are presented as reality. The ideas and philosophy that New Age and UFO proponents have espoused have become accepted "truth."

...so do these also resist the truth: men of corrupt minds, reprobate concerning the faith (2 Tim. 3:8).

Does any Bible-believing Christian really doubt that we are living in the days of which Paul spoke? The evil practices that were once hidden away in a medium's parlor are now attended by multitudes in mass meetings. The mediums have moved uptown and upscale! UFO encounters have become chic! The fact that these things are becoming so popular is both a tragedy and an opportunity. It is tragic that so many people are being deceived and even demon-possessed through these practices. But this age also presents the Church with an opportunity. People are hungry for answers. We have the answers to life's meaning and mankind's future in the Word of God. If the Church will prayerfully begin to share the truth, we can lead many people back from the brink of destruction. This book will hopefully be used to lead many into the kingdom of God.

Sadly, many people seek answers in the wrong places. The answers they are being given by UFO aliens and New Age gurus of various schools of thought are delusions that lead people to the brink of disaster, when mankind will be forced to accept or reject the Antichrist. Those who reject Jesus the Son of God, will readily accept the false christ.

Now the Spirit speaketh expressly, that in the latter times some shall depart from the faith, giving heed to seducing spirits, and doctrines of devils;

Speaking lies in hypocrisy; having their conscience seared with a hot iron ... (1 Tim. 4:1,2).

One UFO author relates the kind of things the "aliens" are teaching. A UFO spirit entity named Semjase said,

Whether we work for God or against God, it matters not, for we are all God — and our forms preserve our Karmic quest in search of the unmanifest.[5] [Author's note: unmanifest is nirvana or brahm.]

This is typical of things being taught by "aliens." There are no absolutes, right or wrong, good or evil in the New Age-UFO religion. When demons and Christ are made to be equally appealing, when people begin to believe that they are God, then Satan can readily turn their minds any way he desires! The Antichrist will not have to coax people who accept such ideas into believing he is the answer — they will receive him with open arms.

Then if any man shall say unto you, Lo, here is Christ, or there; believe it not. For there shall arise false christs, and false prophets, and shall shew great signs and wonders; insomuch that, if it were possible, they shall deceive the very elect (Matt. 24:23-25).

People are being prepared for the great delusion. Many have already been given over to believe the satanic deception through their evil practices and unrepentant hearts. Because the Word of God has been rejected, they are being given over to the deceptive influences of demonic powers. The lie of the New Age-UFOs is leading people to the irrevocable decision they will make when they receive the mark of the Antichrist. (See 2 Thess. 2:8-12 and Rev. 13:16-18; 14:11.)

A Christian can readily see the evil involved in the UFO delusion. Ignorance of this subject is dangerous. Christians need to be aware of what is happening so they can avoid involvement with evil practices; so they can help lead others to truth; so they can enter into prayer and spiritual warfare against this end-time deception.

Even among UFO researchers and proponents there is an uncertainty about what they are encountering. They sense hidden evil in this phenomenon. Brad Steiger writes that,

> *There appear to be those UFO intelligences who are genuinely concerned about our welfare and our spiritual and physical evolution, and there are those who seem largely indifferent to our personal needs and our species' longevity.*[6]

We credit Steiger with honesty and insight. Even so, this is really giving these "aliens" the benefit of the doubt. They not only do not care if we live or die; they are actively seeking our destruction. They are demonic powers whose sole purpose is to work toward the destruction of man and the overthrow of God's kingdom. An even more revealing statement is made by Jacques Vallee at the conclusion of his book *Messengers of Deception:*

> *There is another system. It is sending us messengers of deception. They are not necessarily coming from nearby stars. In terms of the effect on us, it doesn't matter where they come from. I even suspect that "where" and "when" have no meaning here. How could we be alone? The black box of science has stopped ticking. People look upward to the stars in eager expectation.*
>
> *Receiving a visit from outer space sounds almost as comfortable as having a God. Yet we shouldn't rejoice too soon. Perhaps we will get the visitors we deserve.*[7]

There is another "system" and it is not the nearby stars or other planets. The system is the kingdom of darkness, Satan's realm of evil. The effect upon mankind is to prepare humanity for a mass demonic invasion and possession. These messengers of deception are presenting mankind with a false hope. They are promising evolutionary progress to a god-like existence. Instead they will bring people down to destruction. The "where" of the origin of

UFOs and "when" of their appearing are vitally important to humanity. If these are truly demons and they have come for the last days of the age before Jesus returns, then humanity is in the middle of a life-and-death struggle!

People may be comforted with the thought of beings from other planets. They may be looking to the stars. What they will find, however, is not the benevolent alien visitor, but the horrifying truth that Satan himself is coming down to Earth in great fury against mankind. People will eventually get the visitors they deserve because they will reject the offer of God's mercy in Jesus Christ. Having turned from God, they will receive demons and be led to destruction.

Those who will open their hearts to the Lord will have a reason to look to the heavens with hope. Jesus is coming again! Those of us who already believe will go to meet Him in the Rapture. Those who come to faith in Him after the Rapture will look for the time when Jesus returns to end the Antichrist's reign of terror. For those people, who like Vallee, are unsure of who it is that comes in the guise of an alien visitor, there is still time to turn from these messengers of deception to the One true God. The God of the Bible offers truth and life to all who will receive it!

DEMON POSSESSION AND THE PARADIGM SHIFT

The Antichrist will achieve control or influence over most of the people on Earth in the last days. He could not come to power over the world unless he had the help of Satan. This is obvious because even the most popular politician or leader has a sizable opposition that keeps the political leader from unchecked power. It is not through the normal political process that the Antichrist rises to such heights of power. The only explanation for the sudden appearance of a man on the world stage who can gain the following of so many of the people on Earth is that he will have a supernatural power to deceive. Consider the startling fact that he will hold power over most of mankind and will be able to rally the nations to Armageddon. This is not merely a persuasive politician. Some change in mankind's perception of truth and reality must occur for the beast (Antichrist) to gain world rulership. The New Age-UFO religion declares

...humankind will attain a new consciousness, a new awareness, and a higher state — or frequency — of vibration.[8]

Is an as-yet-undetermined someone systematically selecting certain individuals for some worldwide program of psychological conditioning?[9]

We are speaking in terms of a sudden, abrupt changeover in consciousness or modes of thought, concepts, ideas.[10]

As we have observed, this paradigm shift will happen when the Church, the Restrainer, is taken in the Rapture. It will appear that mankind has had a sudden change of perceptions. The intensity of demonic activity will rise suddenly at that time. What is really the cause of the sudden change will be the loosing of evil in full force. Those people who reject truth and have actively sought out evil will be given over to demonic deception and possession. As Paul wrote,

And even as they did not like to retain God in their knowledge, God gave them over to a reprobate mind, to do those things which are not convenient ... (Rom. 1:28).

At the present time some are engaged in evil luciferic practices and some are being possessed as a result. What will happen in the days of the Tribulation will be altogether different in scope and intensity. Then multitudes will be possessed. What would the world be like then? One New Age author ponders this also:

Suppose the plan is to process millions of people

and then at some future date trigger all of these minds at one time. Would we suddenly have a world of saints or would we have a world of armed maniacs shooting one another from bell towers? [11]

Demonic activity is increasing. There is more demon possession now because people engage in practices that invite demonic infestation. One of the authors has interviewed several people who claim to have had personal alien contacts. They all have had prior involvement in some paranormal practice. The rise of both occult activity and UFO activity are no coincidence. They are the same thing. Ruth Montgomery writes of alien "walk-ins" [possession]:

They make up a small but brilliant portion of today's society and they will come in increasing numbers as the earth approaches the shift of the axis during the last part of this century. [12]

They will come in increasing numbers as the time for the earth's shift approaches... [13]

Battle preparation is underway. Any army that plans an invasion pre-positions troops at strategic places to speed the invasion once it begins. This is what Satan is doing. He is placing demonic forces in available individuals in preparation for the lifting of the restraining force that presently holds back his freedom of movement.

The identity of these demonic forces is also known to non-Christians. Even UFO researchers have suspicions as to the real identity of these agents of evil. Steiger observes,

The Ahrimanes, according to Persian and Chaldean tradition, are the fallen angels, who were expelled from heaven for their sins. [14]

Concerning these Ahrimanes, he continues:

A fifth column inside the human mind makes external force unnecessary... [15]

What he is saying is that the aliens may be spirits that are invading Earth to conquer humanity! These aliens are in fact demons. We are already in the early stages of the final war. The Bible speaks of demonic invasion in the last days. In the Book of Revelation, an angel says

And I beheld, and heard an angel flying through the midst of heaven, saying with a loud voice, Woe, woe, woe, to the inhabiters of the earth by reason of the other voices of the trumpet of the three angels, which are yet to sound! (Rev. 8:13).

Three woes are pronounced upon mankind. They follow three trumpets sounded by angels. The first woe is a demonic invasion from the abyss. A horde of demonic forces led by the fallen angel Apollyon is given power to torment men for five months. People will wish to die because of the intense demonic attack. But they cannot die. (See Rev. 9:1-6,10,11.)

In the Gospel of Mark we get a picture of the torment of a person who is demon-possessed. The person who is demon-possessed will try to injure and even kill himself (Mark 5:2-5).

The inhabitants of Earth will be tormented even more intensely. The Restraining force will be gone. Evil powers will have unrestrained access to mankind.

The second woe is the loosing of demonic forces who are stationed at the river Euphrates ready to kill one-third of mankind! Even the carnage of this demonic attack does not cause these people to repent! (See Rev. 9:12-15, 20-21.)

The final of the three woes occurs when Satan himself is cast down to Earth. We all experience his influence in the world today. But he has been limited by the restraint that God has placed upon him. He has not been restricted to dwelling on Earth because he is the prince of the power of the air. His influence has been exercised by subordinates. When he is cast down and restricted to the planet in the last days, his intense fury will be felt by humanity. He will know that only a short time is available to accomplish his scheme before Jesus returns. He will seek to destroy humanity before the Second Coming so that God cannot fulfill all of His promises.

> ...*Woe to the inhabiters of the earth and of the sea! For the devil is come down unto you, having great wrath, because he knoweth that he hath but a short time* (Rev. 12:12).

The hordes of hell and Satan himself, who will possess the Antichrist, will deceive and drive men to the final battle. Those who have taken the mark of the Antichrist will assemble to a valley called in Hebrew "Har Megiddo," the valley at the Mountain of Megiddo, in Israel.

UFO INVASION AND ARMAGEDDON

The battle of Armageddon will be the final attempt of Satan to destroy the human race before Jesus returns. The Antichrist will use the turmoil of the age to draw humanity together in rebellion against God. The wars and horrible catastrophes that will characterize the Tribulation period would under normal circumstances cause people to repent. But during the Tribulation people will be deceived into believing they are threatened by alien invasion. The Antichrist will influence the whole world because of his financial controls. Even so, he will still have opposition in some quarters. However, in spite of infighting, the nations will finally agree to oppose the alien threat. The call to unite is already being sounded. Steiger writes,

> *Again the "angels" i.e. the space intelligences, are speaking to the prophets, the UFO contactees, in order that we might be guided through the difficult period of transition as a new world rises from the ashes of the old.*[16]

Another UFO researcher states,

> *It has been hotly argued that such a menace would offer the last best hope of peace by uniting mankind*

against the danger of destruction by creatures from other planets or from outer space.[17]

The Antichrist will use this threat to persuade people to submit to his rule. They will claim that we need the help of "friendly aliens" to oppose the coming alien invasion (which is really the Second Coming of Christ). If mankind does not submit to the New World Order, the "friendly" aliens will not help mankind!

Assistance on a planetary level will not occur until all nations put a stop to war. These foolish squabbles that are going on in the Middle East must cease. Earth must unite...[18]

Demonic aliens will cause mankind to assemble for the battle of Armageddon. It is interesting that of the three spirits that proceed out of Satan, the Antichrist and the false prophet are frog-like in appearance. If you have seen pictures drawn of the "aliens" that people have seen, you will notice that they often look like humanoid beings with frog-like facial features. The "alien"-demon advisors deceive Earth's leaders into assembling for the battle. (See Rev. 16:12-16.)

The assembled forces will begin the greatest battle ever to take place in the history of the world. In the midst of the confusion of the battle, the heavens will open and Jesus with His army of saints will return. The Antichrist and the armies he has gathered will attempt to fight the Lord, but they will be destroyed by the power of Jesus' spoken word!

And I saw the beast, and the kings of the earth, and their armies, gathered to make war against him that sat on the horse, and against his army. And the beast was taken, and with him the false prophet that wrought miracles before him, with which he deceived them that had received the mark of the beast, and them that worshipped his image. These both were cast alive into a lake of fire burning with brimstone. And the remnant were slain with the sword of him that sat upon the horse, which sword proceeded out of his mouth: and all the fowls were filled with their flesh (Rev. 19:19-21).

Jesus will put an end to the war and the destruction. He will end the Antichrist's reign of terror. He will rescue the remnant of humanity who had not taken the mark of the beast. He will deliver Israel from the threat of annihilation. Some consider Armageddon to be the end of the world. It isn't; it will be the end of war for one thousand years. It will be the end of Satan's ability to hurt mankind for one thousand years. It will be the end of injustice, ecological disasters, immorality, murder, theft, idolatry, and every form of evil. Jesus is coming to rescue His creation from the satanic plot to destroy everything.

And the nations were angry, and thy wrath is come, and the time of the dead, that they should be judged, and that thou shouldest give reward unto thy servants the prophets, and to the saints, and them that fear thy name, small and great; and shouldest destroy them that destroy the earth (Rev. 11:18).

The war will end. The present events that we are witnessing are leading to a terrible time of history. But as believers we can look with hope and faith past the dark days ahead to the bright future of the kingdom of God on Earth! The Earth will be rescued, but not by aliens from other worlds. It will be rescued by the Son of God who created it!

FOOTNOTES

[1]Dr. David A. Lewis, *Prophecy 2000*, New Leaf Press, p.61.

[2]Rev. Robert Shreckhise, *I & II Thessalonians, A Practical Study Guide and Commentary*, unpublished.

[3]Brad Steiger, *The Fellowship*, Ivy Books, p.3.

[4]Jacques Vallee interview, "Vallee Discusses UFO Control System," *Fate Magazine*, p.61.

[5]Brad Steiger, *The Fellowship*, Ivy Books, p.38.

[6]Brad Steiger, *The UFO Abductors*, Berkley Books, p.214.

[7]Jacques Vallee, *Messengers of Deception,* Bantaam, p.246.

[8]Brad Steiger, *The Fellowship*, Ivy Books, p.3.

[9]Ibid., p.48.

[10]Ibid., p.71.

[11]Brad Steiger, *The UFO Abductors*, Berkley Books, p.206.

[12]Ruth Montgomery, *Strangers Among Us,* Fawcett/ Crest, p.16.

[13]Ibid., p.138.

[14]Brad Steiger, *The UFO Abductors*, Berkley Books, p.211.

[15]Ibid. Quoting Trevor James Constable, military and aviation historian, who believes ahrimanic powers are trying to take over the world.

[16]Brad Steiger, *The Fellowship*, Ivy Books, p.194.

[17]J. Allen Hynek and Jacques Vallee, *The Edge of Reality,* Henry Regnery Company, p.158.

[18]Brad Steiger, *The Fellowship*, Ivy Books, p.43.

CHAPTER FOURTEEN

HOLY SPIRIT WORLD LIBERATION

VICTORY IN THE LAST DAYS

We have embarked on a great journey, beginning at Genesis and travelling through the ages into the eternal future of God's kingdom. We have attempted during the journey to offer a cohesive explanation for the puzzling UFO phenomenon. Now we will consider a plan for end-time victory, an agenda for dealing with UFOs and other deceptive philosophies that prevail in our time of history.

THE DECEPTION OF UFOs

We are convinced that the UFO phenomenon is part of the end-time demonic delusion that Satan is using to prepare the world for the Antichrist. We have demonstrated that the UFO phenomenon involves deceptive brainwashing techniques. Evil, spiritual entities are using powers they retain as fallen angels to create the illusion of reality, and thereby transform mankind's perception of reality the paradigm shift to which the New Age movement is constantly referring. This paradigm shift is due to demonic control and influence.

Demons, as fallen angels, apparently retain great powers, such as the manipulation and restructuring of matter, as well as the ability to influence or control

*human consciousness and experience through classic
possession or by direct psychic implantation of a set of
experiences.* [1]

The deception has the purpose of destroying the
knowledge of the truth of God's Word. We have shown the
animosity that UFO entities have toward the Bible. They
do not want people to accept the literal truth of the Word
of God. They replace the biblical world-view with the occult
world-view. They replace God with a universal mind. They
replace salvation with reincarnation and evolution. The
purpose of this satanic scheme is to push mankind over the
brink to destruction!

*...some of Satan's work is dedicated to disorganizing
God's kingdom and some to organizing his own. He
intends to disrupt the true knowledge and worship of
God through destruction, confusion and lies. He works
to establish the structure of his influence both positively
and negatively, by dispensing favors to some and
intimidating others.* [2]

In the last few years there has been another wave of
UFO activity. During the 1950s and 1970s there was a
periodic spurt in this activity. With increase in New Age
practices in the last ten years, there has been a
corresponding increase in UFO sightings and other strange
occurrences. We believe that the 1990s will be a very active
time for this deception as the New Age movement gains
acceptance by more people. There is a purpose in this
periodic increase of UFO activity:

*We are dealing with a control system ... the best
schedule of reinforcement is one that combines
periodicity with unpredictability ... I suggest that it is
human belief that is being controlled and conditioned
... UFOs ... are the means through which man's
concepts are being rearranged ... with every new wave
of UFOs the social impact becomes greater...* [3]

The mechanisms of control, complex as they are, have seemingly gone into high gear during the last decade or so, and are communicating variations on the theme of a basically occult world-view to the unregenerate mass of global humanity through a bewildering diversity of means and media.[4]

As the end draws nearer, we expect that there will be an ever increasing rise in the frequency of UFO sightings and close encounters with ETIs. These will become the subject of increasing news coverage leading to a general acceptance of UFOs and ETIs.

We believe that the thousands of cases of transformation represent one aspect of the ultimate purpose of UFOs. They are part of a plan to deliberately move significant portions of an entire culture, or world, into acceptance or involvement in the occult, and a collective alteration in world view. This is preparatory for and necessary to the events surrounding the rise of the Antichrist.[5]

Those who accept these phenomena as reality will also inevitably accept the occultic world-view that the UFO entities promote. Hearts and minds are being transformed and prepared for the coming occultic rule of the Antichrist, the man of sin!

What we must be careful to note is that there is a logical inconsistency in accepting these beings as "higher beings." Their actions and words reveal them to be anything but advanced and perfected "space brothers":

Aside from all the conjectured prohibitions against the likelihood of contact with unfallen extraterrestrials, the fact is that the actual cases of reported contact suggest that they are anything but unfallen. Abduction, psychological and psychic manipulation and violence, sexual assault, and physical attack are not uncommon features of UFO contact ... We would hardly expect an unfallen people to speak to us in terms of "having evolved" or having solved some pre-existent problems, as though an encouragement to evolution is all we need to hear. An unfallen race would not have had pre-existent problems. Moreover, their message would definitely not pander to the very human positivism which Christ declares to be vain.[6]

This all points to the demonic nature of these beings and the satanic origin of their "plan."

The whole point is that these beings are deceiving people with their illusions of reality. Mankind is being duped by the greatest con-artist of all time. Jesus describes Satan this way:

...the devil ... He was a murderer from the beginning, and abode not in the truth, because there is no truth in him. When he speaketh a lie, he speaketh of his own: for he is a liar, and the father of it (John 8:44).

The thief cometh not, but for to steal, and to kill, and to destroy ... (John 10:10).

But Jesus said of himself, "...I am come that they might have life, and that they might have it more abundantly." Paul wrote,

But evil men and seducers shall wax worse and worse, deceiving, and being deceived (2 Tim. 3:13).

Many people are in danger from this deception. Is there an antidote? Do we have the answer? How can we lead people back from the brink of destruction and resist the evil forces that seek our annihilation? Our answer is that they can find life in Jesus — who gives life that is eternal.

ANTIDOTE FOR DECEPTION

People are looking for a connection to the spiritual nature of man. In our modern culture people have become fragmented and confused. They want to find an answer for their existence and a hope for the future. They want to find a foundation upon which to build their lives. They are looking for a central truth or cause to which they can commit themselves. Drugs, illicit sex, money, and success have left people empty. In the search for something that satisfies this longing and fills the emptiness, many are turning to the New Age and to UFOs.

The spirituality that the New Age/UFO religion offers is a false hope. It is based upon subjective human feelings and observations that are being manipulated by demonic forces. The psychic implantation of deceptive experiences is changing the way they perceive reality. What they experience is a real experience — deceptive and manipulative in character. It is not, however, an experience of reality. It is an illusion of reality used solely for the purpose of convincing people to turn away from the Creator.

The reality of the UFO experience is an encounter with incredibly evil and malevolent demonic entities that want the destruction of humanity.

The New Age/UFO follower thinks he has found the connection for which he has sought. He thinks he has found a spirituality that will satisfy all his longings. The truth is that these experiences only bring bondage and eventual destruction. On the other hand, there are many people in the New Age movement who may yet be reached with the truth of the gospel.

The Lord is not slack concerning his promise, as some men count slackness; but is long-suffering to us-ward, not willing that any should perish, but that all should come to repentance (2 Peter 3:9).

The Lord does not want the destruction of anyone. Each human being has a choice to make. We believe that many within the New Age/UFO religion may yet choose the Lord Jesus Christ if the message is lovingly presented to them. It is for these people that our prayers must be offered and to whom our witness must be given.

The Bible offers a true spirituality that is based on demonstrable, objective, historical fact.

God offers truth to us in the Bible. He offers us forgiveness and eternal life. He offers us an ongoing, personal relationship of love and life!

God loves us! He doesn't want us to perish, to be destroyed. The antidote for the New Age/UFO delusion is the gospel of Jesus Christ. He is the only hope for the human race.

What prevents you from asking Jesus to become your Saviour right now? You can pray the following prayer:

Dear God, I recognize that I have sinned. I have broken the commandments of Your Word, the Bible. I have been neglecting Your offer of forgiveness and eternal life. I confess this to You. I ask You to forgive me because of the price that Jesus Your Son paid when He died for my sins.

Lord Jesus, I ask You to come in to my heart and to live in my life from this day onward. I give myself to You. I ask You to fill my life with the power of the Holy Spirit. I receive Your forgiveness according to the promise of Your Word. I thank You for my new life. I thank You for Your power in the Holy Spirit. My whole heart praises You for the eternal life You have given me! Praise to God the Father and glory to Jesus Christ His Son! Amen.

Once a person has accepted the truth of the Bible and has asked Jesus to become his personal Saviour, there is the possibility that recurring, residual problems may trouble the former New Age/UFO follower. A person who has opened his life to any kind of occult involvement will often find that nightmares, physical problems, or other symptoms of demonic attack continue. It will be necessary in such cases to renounce the New Age/UFO religion and to continually submit to Jesus Christ as Lord.

How is a renunciation made? We will give you a sample of this, but you can say the same thing in your own words. This is not a prayer. It is a legal statement, a vow, made before God, the angels of heaven, and, if possible, a couple of dedicated Christian friends.

I renounce all involvement in the New Age, UFO, and occult practices in which I formerly participated. I renounce them as evil in God's sight. I recognize the great sin involved in these practices, and I am genuinely sorry that I ever engaged in them.

I turn away from them. I vow to destroy all charms, power objects, books, and occult paraphernalia in my possession. I promise to never again return to these activities. I hereby forsake all involvement in any such practices for the rest of my life.

I thank God for delivering me from the darkness of these things. I commit myself to serving the Lord Jesus Christ, to the best of my ability, and by His grace, for the rest of my life. May His name be praised forever!

Once you have made this statement before God, the angels, and Christian witnesses, and have genuinely turned from these evil practices, you have broken every legal right that Satan ever had upon you. Since we are engaged in spiritual warfare, God counsels us:

Submit yourselves therefore to God. Resist the devil, and he will flee from you. Draw nigh to God, and he will draw nigh to you... (James 4:7,8).

Who hath delivered us from the power of darkness, and hath translated us into the kingdom of his dear Son: In whom we have redemption through his blood, even the forgiveness of sins... (Col. 1:13,14).

STANDING WATCH IN PRAYER AND SPIRITUAL WARFARE

A very necessary part of end-time Christian responsibility is spiritual warfare. Spiritual warfare is not only prayer; it is also resistance. We pray to God the Father in the name of Jesus Christ our Lord. We pray for our brothers and sisters. We pray for the gospel's expansion in the world. We pray for the conversion of the lost. We pray for our nation and our leaders so that we can continue to freely preach the truth. We also resist the spirit of the Antichrist in the world. Resistance is not prayer. It is an open act of restraint against the enemy. When we pray, we bow our heads before God in respect and reverence. When we resist Satan, we stand up straight and with our eyes open. We do not revere the enemy — we fight him in the Lord's authority and power!

PRAYER:

Almighty God, we come to You in the mighty name of the Lord Jesus Christ. Grant to us the authority of believers to resist the powers of darkness. We plead the power of Jesus' shed blood as our covering. We claim the promise of Jesus that the gates of hell shall not prevail against the Church. We now join together in attacking the gates of hell and the powers of the Antichrist. Let our liberties be preserved so that the gospel may be freely declared.

RESISTANCE:

Note that this is not a prayer. We do not pray to Satan. But, as Jesus did in the wilderness, we authoritatively speak a rebuke to him.

Satan, I join my brothers and sisters in Christ to resist you in the name of our Lord Jesus Christ. The Lord rebuke you, Satan. You have no power over us. We come against the powers of the Antichrist in the name of the Son of God. We resist the evil powers of darkness in the name of the Lord Jesus Christ. We come against you, Satan, in the power of Jesus' shed blood. You are a defeated enemy and you must yield to our attack. Christ has conquered you.

WE RESIST the power of the Antichrist as it is mani-fested in government, religion, economics, science, communications, education, art, entertainment, and other realms.

Satan, we drive you back into a position of powerlessness and defeat. In Jesus' name we bind the UFO deceivers. We restrain and rebuke the powers of the Antichrist in other nations. We rebuke the demonic forces that try to hinder the work of missions. You must now free their hands, in Jesus' name.

PRAYER:

Heavenly Father, in the name of Jesus Christ, protect the brothers and sisters who have joined the restraining force. Amen.

For further information and literature about the "Holy Spirit World Liberation" force, request a complimentary prayer packet. Write to:

Dr. David A. Lewis
P.O. Box 11115, Springfield, MO 65808

If you are just now accepting Christ as Saviour, ask for the free redemption packet.

David A. Lewis Ministries, Inc. publishes a quarterly paper, *The Prophecy Intelligence Digest*. Request a complimentary one-year mailing of this paper.

VICTORY AHEAD!

There is potential for great victory for the Church in the last days of this present age. Part of our purpose in writing this book is to cry aloud and warn the Church of the coming battles that we face. We are watchmen on the walls of the Church who blow the trumpet of the Lord and sound the alarm in His holy mountain (Joel 2:1), saying to believers,

The day of the Lord is coming! Get ready! Prepare for battle, for the end is drawing near! We are sons of Issachar (1 Chron. 12.32) who have "understanding of the times, to know what Israel ought to do..." We are giving you insight into the age in which we live. We are giving you a battle plan for victory. We are proclaiming in the name of the Lord that the Church can stand and be mighty in the Lord's power!

It is our desire that after having read this book, your awareness will be stirred. We hope that you will be moved to action. From all indications the age in which we live is the Rapture Age. We are on the threshold of the greatest adventure of all adventures. In the next few hours or months or years that are left before Jesus returns, there is much to be done. There are many people who need to hear the truth of the good news of Jesus Christ. Our prayer is that you will dedicate the rest of your life to serving the God of Creation in the power of His Spirit through Jesus Christ His Son.

FOOTNOTES

[1]*SCP Journal,* August 1977, Vol.1 No.2, "UFOs — Is Science Fiction Coming True?" p.19.

[2]Ibid., p.22.

[3]Ibid., p. 22, Quoting Jacques Vallee

[4]Ibid., p.22.

[5]Ibid., p.23.

[6]*SCP Journal,* August 1977, Vol.1 No.2, "UFOs and the Logic of Discernment," p.28.

APPENDIX

Various new schemes of evolution have been proposed since Darwin's time. But they all relate to the same basic world-view. One such theory is Dr. Fox's theory of inert matter turning into simple life forms. His experiments at the University of Miami have attempted to show that a chemical soup can react spontaneously, combining into primitive life forms. The results have been touted as proof of evolution. The claim has even been made that he produced a living virus. However, the result of his experiments is far from proving evolution. He has simply been able to cause some basic compounds to form an amino acid. There are hundreds of amino acids in one DNA chain. In addition, they must be combined in a specific order. If too many are out of place or missing, the DNA will not replicate properly. A DNA chain that has mutated too much will cause rapid degeneration with an end-result of the eventual extinction of a life form. (All true mutations are degenerative to a species.) Without DNA replication, life cannot exist!

The mathematical probabilities against DNA forming spontaneously are so great as to preclude it. For instance, consider the following quotes:

In the October 1969 issue of Nature *magazine, UFO, APPENDIX Page 2, Dr. Frank Salisbury of Utah State University, currently on leave at the Division of Biomedical and Environmental research at the U.S. Atomic Energy Commission, examined the chance of one of the most basic chemical reactions for the continuation of life taking place. This reaction involves the formation of a specific DNA molecule ... He concluded that the chances of just this one tiny DNA molecule coming into existence over four billion years, with conditions just right, on just one of these almost infinite number of hospitable planets, including the earth, was one chance in 10415.*[1]

Dr. Emile Borel, one of the world's greatest experts on mathematical probability, formulated a basic law of probability. It states that the occurrence of any event where the chances are beyond one in 10^{50} — a much smaller figure than what we have been dealing with — is an event that we can state with certainty will never happen — no matter how much time is allotted, no matter how many conceivable opportunities could exist for the event to take place. In other words, life by chance is mathematically impossible on Earth or any place else.[2]

Another article related that three prominent evolutionists — astronomers Sir Fred Hoyle and Chandra Wickramasinghe and paleontologist Colin Patterson — have come to reject evolution.

Hoyle and Wickramasinghe said that life can't be explained by any random process, "Once we see that the probability of life originating at random is so utterly minuscule as to make it absurd, it becomes sensible to think that the favorable properties of physics on which life depends are in every respect deliberate, and it is almost inevitable that our own measure of intelligence must reflect higher intelligence even to the limit of God." Although they had been atheists and resisted this vigorously, they said they finally came to believe in God as the only possible explanation of the origin of life.[3]

(Patterson questioning...) *"Can you tell me anything*

you know about evolution, any one thing that is true? I tried that question on the geology staff at the Field Museum of Natural History, and the only answer I got was silence. " He tried it on the Evolutionary Morphology Seminar at the University of Chicago, a very prestigious body of evolutionists, and all he got there "was silence for a long time and eventually one person said, I do know one thing — it ought not to be taught in high school."[4]

Another theory has been to claim that spores from other worlds seeded our planet either by directly being blown here on cosmic winds or through traveling on meteors. The problem with this idea is that radiation would have killed all such life long before it could reach Earth. If it were a radiation resistant life-form, then where is this radiation resistance in every other life-form? The spores' DNA would have carried this characteristic and passed it on to one degree or another to every other life form — if we use the evolutionists' reasoning about genetic mutations. In addition, the origin of these space-spores must be explained. (In the same way must the origin of space-beings also be explained.) This only pushes back the ultimate question of origins one step — it does not deal with it. These and every other naturalistic explanation for life have failed to show positive results.

Every evolutionary model, including the UFO model, must as a necessity have an old universe and Earth to be logical in their correlations of ideas. In speaking of the evolutionary time frame, we must realize that they theorize in terms of billions of years! Evidence shows that the universe is younger by many orders of magnitude. One scientist, Thomas G. Barnes of the University of Texas at El Paso, author of a study in the decay of the Earth's magnetic fields, writes,

"There is nothing more devastating to the doctrine of evolution than the scientific evidence of a young Earth age. That evidence is provided by the rapid depletion of the energy in the Earth's main magnet, its electromagnetic dipole magnet in the conductive core of the Earth."[5]

In an article concerning evolution in the magazine *Christianity Today,* there were several scientific reasons given to reject evolution. The reasons are adapted from the article and summarized as follows:

1. Receding moon. The distance of the Moon from the Earth would be much greater if the vast time spans dictated by evolution were true. The Moon recedes from the Earth as time passes. If the present rate is multiplied by the evolutionary time frame, the distance would be much greater than it is presently.

2. Shape of the Earth. The spin rate of the Earth is slowing. If the present decay of the rate is extrapolated back one billion years, the spin rate would be twice as fast. A molten Earth spinning at such a rate would have a noticeable bulge in the middle, which does not exist.

3. Lunar dust depth. The depth of the dust on the moon should be many times deeper than it is if the universe were as old as evolutionists claim.

4. Radiometric evidence of a young Earth. Polonium-218 decayed left halos in granite found deep within the Earth's crust. The half life of Polonium-218 is only three minutes. For it to be able to leave radioactive signatures in the granite, the granite must have cooled very rapidly.

5. Magnetic evidence of a young Earth. The rate of decay in the Earth's magnetic field indicates a very young Earth of only a few thousand years.

6. Shrinking sun. The rate of the sun's shrinking is five feet per hour. This puts an upper limit on the age of the sun at approximately 10 million years. This does not rule out a much younger sun.[6]

A most astounding new discovery pointing to a young creation is found in Lambert Dolphin's book, *Jesus: Lord of Time and Space.* In his book Dr. Lambert writes about the theory proposed by Trevor Norman and Barry Setterfield of Flinders University of South Australia. Their study in the velocity of light has shaken the world of science to its roots. They have shown strong evidence from statistical studies that the speed of light is not a constant. In fact it has slowed down by many orders of magnitude over the time since the beginning (more than 1×10^7 times slower today than at creation). According to the mathematical calculations of Norman and Setterfield, the age of the universe in 1958 was 6,083 years old! Not only does the direct indication of the universe's age come from the mathematical calculation of a curve of decay in the speed of light (thus going backward a mathematical approximation of the maximum original speed and the date of creation), the decaying speed of light changes the rates of radioactive decay.

Radiometric dating has long been a standby proof that evolutionists have used to indicate the ancient origin of the universe. Consider that if the speed of light was 1×10^6 times faster at the beginning, then the rate of decay for every radioactive isotope used in radiometric dating would be $(1 \times 10^7)^2$ faster than it is now. This is true because of Einstein's equation, $E = MC^2$. Radioactive decay is directly proportional to the square of the speed of light! Therefore all radiometric dates for Earth's original formations would be 1×10^{14} less ancient (10 to the 7th power squared = 10 to the 14th power) than claimed by evolutionists. In addition to this, dating methods before 3500 B.C. are very inaccurate. One author writes,

Carbon dating can be shown to be somewhat accurate for one half-life — that is, approximately five and a half thousand years — for there are written records that can be put alongside dates for that period. Beyond that period dating is an open question for there simply are not absolutes against which specific dates can be fixed with accuracy.[7]

So, if the above ideas are true, there is no reasonable way that science can demonstrate an old universe. An example of the inaccuracy of radiometric dating occurred when rock formations in Hawaii were dated, using potassium to argon dating, at one-half million years.

Actually, these volcanic rocks are known to have been formed only two hundred years ago. In contrast to this, true science is repeatedly demonstrating the accuracy of Genesis as a record of the creation.

FOOTNOTES

[1]John Weldon with Zola Levitt, *UFOs — What on Earth is Happening?* Harvest House, pp.154-155.

[2]Ibid., p.155.

[3]*Pulpit Helps* newspaper, quoting February 1982 article by Luther D. Sunderland in Bible Science Newsletter.

[4]Ibid.

[5]Warren H. Johns, *Ministry* magazine January 1984, article entitled, "Controversy Over Paleomagnetic Dating," p.25.

[6]Thomas G. Barnes, *Christianity Today* magazine October 8, 1982, "Evidence Points to a Recent Creation," pp.34-36.

[7]Clifford Wilson, Ph.D., *Crash Go the Chariots,* A Lancer Book, p.84.